Walks in Ancient Lakeland

Robert Harris

Published by Sigma Leisure – an imprint of
Sigma Press, 1 South Oak Lane, Wilmslow,
Cheshire SK9 6AR, England.

British Library Cataloguing in Publication Data
A CIP record for this book is available from the British Library.

ISBN: 1-85058-763-9

Typesetting and Design by: Sigma Press, Wilmslow, Cheshire.

Cover photograph: Castlerigg Stone Circle *(Ikon Imaging)*
Cover design: Design House, Marple Bridge

Maps and illustrations: Robert Harris
Location map: Morag Perrott

Printed by: MFP Design and Print

Disclaimer: the information in this book is given in good faith and is believed to be correct at the time of publication. No responsibility is accepted by either the author or publisher for errors or omissions, or for any loss or injury howsoever caused. Only you can judge your own fitness, competence and experience.

Preface

This is a book of walks in and around the Lake District which visit the sites and monuments left to us by the people who lived there before the coming of the Romans. These people, our ancestors, were the first to settle and farm the land, in the Late Neolithic and Bronze Ages, and were the first to build structures which still survive today. Their great stone circles, standing stones and burial cairns still decorate these beautiful hills, and their ancient trackways still link their scattered settlements.

The walks vary from as little as two miles, to some of ten miles or more. Some are down in the valleys beside our modern farms and villages, while others are high on wild and remote fells. Each visits sites which give us some insight into our ancestors' distant lives and often follow their trackways and trading routes. Each walk is circular, starting and finishing at a place convenient to reach by car. Most of the routes are pleasant in themselves, but I hope the historical element not only adds interest, but also gives a purpose and focus to each walk.

I have divided the area into two sectors, Eastern and Western Lakeland, rather as it would have been in Neolithic times. The dividing line runs roughly along the great valley systems which link Bassenthwaite, Thirlmere and Windermere. In ancient times, this line separated the two important settlement areas of south-west and north-east Lakeland with the high ridges of Helvellyn and High Street between them. The only major site which lies close to the line is Castlerigg stone circle, and for the purposes of this book I have included it in the eastern sector as it is geographically closer to the sites around Penrith than those to the south.

When taking the higher level walks, always follow the usual rules of mountain safety: go properly equipped, carry a map and compass (and know how to use them) and be prepared for sudden changes in the weather. The maps in the book are sketch maps only. For greater accuracy and detail, consult the appropriate O.S. Outdoor Leisure sheet. The walks follow public rights of way wherever possible, but some of the sites are on private land. Treat all the land with respect and if in doubt always ask permission.

Equally important, respect these ancient and sacred sites, many of which have survived for almost five thousand years. They are our link with our history and they reach out to us from the deep abyss of the past. Treat them with the respect they deserve and help to preserve them for future generations to enjoy.

I would like to thank Rowenna, Mairi, Bethan, Chris, Howard, Phil and Lynne for their company on the walks, and for their help and their hospitality. Lastly, I hope you derive as much pleasure from visiting and exploring these ancient places as I have.

Robert Harris

Dedication

To my Dad,
who still stands beside me,
though he has stepped
beyond the stones.

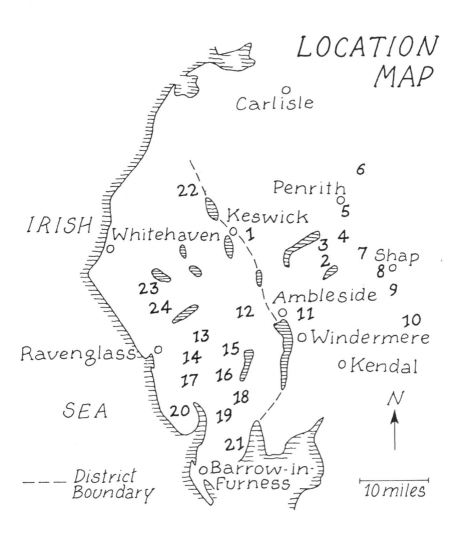

LOCATION MAP

IRISH

SEA

Carlisle

Penrith
6
5

22
Keswick
Whitehaven
1

3 4
2
7 Shap
8 9

23
24
12
Ambleside
11
10
Windermere

13
Ravenglass
14 15
16
17
Kendal

18
20 19
N

21
Barrow-in-Furness

10 miles

--- District
Boundary

Key to symbols used on maps

❘	Standing Stone
⁞⁞	Stone Circle
∴	Cairn Circle
⬭	Henge
▲	Cairn or Tumulus
⚇	Ringcairn
☼	Encampment or Enclosure
⋒	Burial Chamber
◀	Longcairn
◞◞◞	Stone Row
◦◦◦	Clearance Cairns
◀	Axe Factory Site

Contents

Introduction

As the great ice sheets of the last Ice Age retreated about 10,000 years ago, the area we now know as the Lake District would have resembled Iceland or Greenland as they are today. Remnants of ice caps would have survived on the higher mountains and the valleys would have been barren and boulder-strewn wastelands, largely devoid of life.

Over the following millennia, the last of the ice would have melted and simple plants and animals begun to recolonize the wilderness. As soil began to develop and the climate improved, the fells below the highest peaks would have come to look like the landscape as we know it today. A scattering of oak, willow and birch trees would have been interspersed with more open areas of heath and moorland plants.

Into this landscape, animals spread from the south. Bears, wolves, deer, wild cattle and pigs flourished in increasing numbers. With the animals came people, spreading along the coasts and up the major river valleys. They would have lived by hunting and fishing and collecting berries, nuts and shellfish, and for several thousand years they would have made little impact on the landscape. They probably led a nomadic existence, living in simple shelters or skin tents and travelling with the game they relied on for food.

Whether the change from this way of life to a more sedentary farming one happened gradually, with ideas slowly being passed on and adopted from community to community, or suddenly with an influx of new people migrating from the south, is not clear. However, we do know that by about 4,000 BC people were living in the area and using the woodland for timber, keeping animals for food and growing basic crops on land cleared of trees. Hunting and gathering would probably still have been important as ways of supplementing their diet.

Their homes would have become more permanent, but it is likely that seasonal movements would still have been necessary to make the best use of grazing land for the animals, and to avoid the harsh weather of the upland winters.

It is during this period, called the Late Neolithic, that the first major changes to the natural landscape would have taken place. As the population grew, larger tracts of woodland were cleared for farmland and for timber to use for buildings, fencing and fuel. The first structures built for purposes other than shelter appeared at about this time. These early ceremonial constructions are known as henges, and were circles or enclosures of large vertical timbers often set within a ditch and surrounded by a bank.

The exact purpose of these structures is still not clear but their size indicates the gathering together of people for ceremonies of some kind and it is likely they were of a religious nature. Several henges can still be seen in the Lake District, notably Mayburgh and King Arthur's Table near Penrith.

Mayburgh henge

In southern England, very large encampments, known as causewayed camps, also date from this period. Their purpose does not appear to be defensive, because of the many entrances that each one had, and they were probably meeting or trading places. The camp just to the north of Great Urswick in southern Lakeland could possibly be an example of this type of site.

It was at about this time, roughly 3,000 BC, that the building of the megalithic monuments began. Stones replaced the earlier timbers in the henges, and the first of the great circles were built. These were the large circles, of which Cumbria has so many fine examples. Their size indicates that they were built and used by large communities, for each must have been a huge undertaking for a people who had only wooden, stone and bone tools to work with. Each stone, sometimes weighing many tons had to be quarried and shaped before being transported and erected. The largest stone at Castlerigg is estimated to weigh sixteen tons and would have needed many men to manoeuvre it into position. They were sometimes built on specially levelled platforms and were often carefully aligned so that major stones acted as markers for the rising or setting of the sun and moon on significant dates in the calendar.

Some of these great circles appear to have been sited on or close to prominent hills or near to important springs. Perhaps these natural features were the focal points of earlier communities and the building of ceremonial sites close by is an indication of their continuing importance. The natural rock outcrop on Eskdale Moor is a good example, with three stone circles sited just below it.

It has been suggested that these early rings were meeting places where valuable commodities such as stone axes were bought and exchanged. The 'axe factory' at Langdale and the smaller ones on Great Gable and Scafell were in full production during this period and several axes from there have been discovered at Castlerigg. Some of these axes have been found, highly polished and unused as if they were symbols of status rather than mere tools.

In this late Stone Age period, the great circles of Castlerigg and Sunkenkirk, Meg and her Daughters and Gamelands were built. Their builders must have lived either in large tribal groups or at least gathered together at certain times of the year in large numbers. They must have had enough time free from food production to spare for the huge task of constructing the circles.

The beautiful carvings on some stones also indicate a society where

culture and art played a significant role. A stone at Little Meg has typical spirals and concentric circles carved into it. In Scotland, strange stone balls were intricately carved, although whether these were purely for art or for some other purpose is unclear.

As well as being skilful craftsmen in stone, they had also developed a high degree of skill with clay. Fine examples of beautifully decorated pottery have been discovered in Cumbria, such as the small collared urn found at the Druids' Circle near Ulverston. So these people were not savages as is commonly assumed, but counted amongst their number skilled potters and artists, stone masons and engineers. This was a society capable of organizing large numbers of people to achieve a common goal.

Their dead, buried in longbarrows and chambered long cairns, were not individual interments, for the bones of many people are usually found mixed together and jumbled up. In the great longbarrows of southern England, many skulls and leg bones were discovered inside the chambers but with other bones missing. Perhaps the dead were exposed to the elements first, and only selected bones were interred in the barrows with their ancestors.

Few examples of such chambered cairns have survived in the Lake District, although a large, tree-covered longbarrow can be found right beside the M6 just to the south of Penrith, and another near Crosby Ravensworth further east. A ruined burial chamber on the limestone scars to the north of Great Urswick is the only remaining exposed dolmen in the district.

As the Stone Age merged into the Bronze Age about 4,000 years ago, the large circles would still have been in use as they had for almost a thousand years. Individuals were by now being buried separately, sometimes in cairns built inside the older circles such as at Castlerigg. Burial cairns are to be found all over Lakeland in many shapes and forms. Fine examples of ringcairns and kerbed cairns, round cairns and long cairns are scattered across the uplands, some with stone cists still surviving within them.

New circles were built, not the huge ones of earlier days, but smaller ones with smaller stones. This seems to indicate a break up of society from large tribal communities to smaller groupings requiring smaller ceremonial places. Possibly just large extended families lived and farmed an area and built their own places of worship.

It is during this period that the paired circles were built. Eskdale Moor has several fine pairs of circles barely twenty metres apart. Other strange arrangements of stones remain from this time such as the ruined stone rows of Lacra, near Millom, whose purpose is still a mystery.

The upland moors were farmed intensively, as can be seen from the number of clearance cairns which are still scattered across the fells close to ancient stone monuments, and we assume that the people lived close by. Settlement sites are to be found on many of the low fells, but few have been excavated or dated accurately and may be more associated with later periods.

Metal working had by this time reached the area, and bronze tools and ornaments were cast using copper ore, probably from local mines, and tin from the south-west of England. These metal products would have been important status symbols, helping to create an elite in society, which is also indicated by the increase in high status, individual burials from this period. Grave goods such as tools and hunting weapons, food and drinking vessels were put inside the cists of important individuals. There is also evidence that flowers were placed beside their bodies in a custom which has carried on to the present day.

Burial customs continued to change and cremations became more common. Significantly, the old stone circles continued to be used for these interments, underlining their continuing importance as sacred sites.

As the Bronze Age drew to a close about 2,800 years ago, the population was increasing rapidly and with it came added pressure on land to farm. The Iron Age brought with it a fierce tribalism and battles for land

and power. Huge defensive forts were constructed, sometimes on the same hills as the much older causewayed camps. With the coming of iron, the age of the megaliths waned and slowly died, the weather deteriorated and the people retreated from the higher fells. The circles and stones were abandoned and the old Gods gradually forgotten.

Many people see the late Neolithic and early Bronze Age as a 'Golden Period', without wars or strife, when food was plentiful, land was free and the weather was good. In reality, it was probably as hard as any period of our history. But it was our history! These were our ancestors, and although Christianity has labelled them as godless and wicked savages these 'heathens', were in fact, just ordinary people who worshipped, not in churches, but out on the heath under the open sky.

We can never relive the past, but we can revisit the places where it took place. We can see the same views, experience the same atmosphere and touch the same stones as our forefathers. And of those ancient people, what became of them? The answer is that something of them still exists, not just in their sacred places, but within all of us. We all retain, often unknowingly, beliefs and feelings and customs that date back to those distant times.

They lived lives, probably shorter and more brutal than ours, but perhaps also more simple. They were more attuned to the earth, the sky, to the seasons and the weather and quite possibly they experienced pleasures long lost to modern man.

In many of us there is a growing feeling that we have become too divorced from the land and that we are the worse for it. The seasons pass us by almost unnoticed, the sky is dimmed by the bright lights of civilization, and the feel of real earth beneath our feet has become almost a novelty. As we find ourselves more and more encapsulated within our air-conditioned, sympathetically lit, twenty-four hour a day existences, we seem to be missing out on so much which enriched our lives.

To find again some balance, many of us need to escape occasionally from our normal routines and search for something else. We feel the need to walk upon the hills and go to those wild places that to our ancestors were special, to replant our roots, once again, deep within the ground and, hopefully, feel the steadier for it.

Eastern Lakeland

The main entrance to Castlerigg circle is formed by two large stones, which from within the ring, frame the craggy summit of Blencathra beyond.

1. Castlerigg

Approx. distance: 5 miles

Approx. time: 3 hours

Starting point: Dale Bottom G.R.294217

O.S. Outdoor Leisure Sheet: 6

Grid references: Castlerigg stone circle G.R.292237; outlying stone G.R.291236

Castlerigg circle can be easily reached by car and a one minute walk, but to appreciate it fully it needs to be seen in the context of the surrounding landscape. This can best be done from the hills to the east, and our walk takes you over these before dropping down to the stones.

As you leave the main road at Causeway Foot, a narrow lane leads over the stream and through a campsite into the tiny hamlet of Dale Bottom. The quiet lane eastwards crosses the wide, flat valley of Naddle Beck before climbing up onto the lower slopes of High Rigg. For a short distance it contours around the hillside, before climbing steeply to the col between High Rigg and its lower outlying hill of Low Rigg.

The little church of St. John's in the Vale sits in a beautiful position looking out over the valley of St. John's Beck to the east. From the church, a path takes you north, up onto the moorlands of Low Rigg. The close-cropped turf is interspersed with patches of cotton grass, and tiny yellow tormentil shines out beside the path.

Where the footpath crosses the wall it is possible to scramble up steeply onto the top of the hill. This is a marvellous place, high and rocky, with views out in all directions to the mountains which seem to ring it. Below, Castlerigg stone circle is at the centre of it all, Blencathra and Skiddaw to the north, Helvellyn to the south-east and Grasmoor, hazily purple, in the far distance.

The circle, tiny from this distance, sits on a low ridge, like the hub of a great wheel rimmed by the high mountains. The sky arcs like an enormous dome from horizon to far horizon. This scene, one of the finest in Lakeland, will have changed little in the last five thousand years. Perhaps someone sat on the rocky top of Low Rigg all those years ago and realized that there could be no finer place to build a great circle than on the low hills above Naddle Beck.

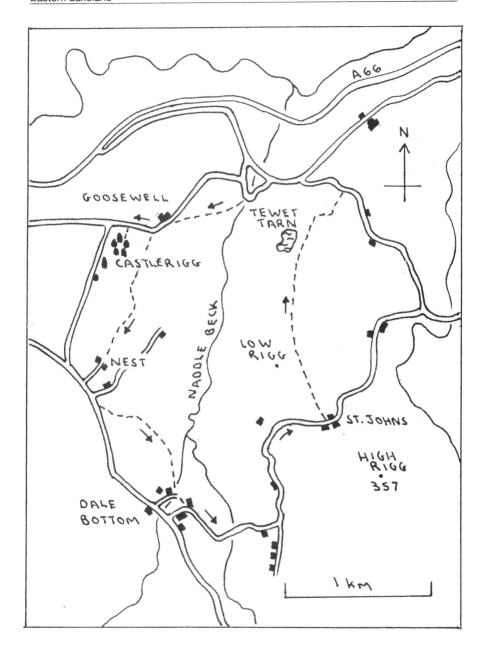

'The largest stone of Castlerigg stands beside its unique rectangular enclosure. In the distance, Helvellyn peers over the shoulder of Lower Man, and looks down upon the circle.'

Scrambling back down from the top, a small marshy area is passed before the path is regained. Here amongst the sphagnum moss, purple spikes of lousewort rise between the reeds and the tiny carnivorous sundew plants hide, with their sticky leaves open expectantly.

The route follows the path northwards past Tewet Tarn before dropping down again to the lane. Where the road crosses once more over the beck, now wide and weedy beneath the bridge, a path climbs up across the fields to Goosewell Farm. From here, a short walk along the lane leads to a path across the field to the circle.

This is one of the oldest circles in the Lake District. Like the other large rings at Sunkenkirk and Long Meg and Her Daughters, it was built about 4500 years ago in the late Neolithic period. Its size indicates that it must have been an important site and would have served a large local community, but surprisingly there are few other sites remaining in the area. Perhaps, because it is a relatively low-lying area and is heavily farmed, all other traces have been destroyed. About thirty-nine stones remain in what is Lakeland's most famous ring, and each one has its own individual shape and size. Some have fallen and some have been taken away but it still manages to retain its powerful aura, and its position within the landscape is unique. The main entrance is formed by two large stones, which from within the ring, frame the craggy summit of Blencathra beyond. Another entrance lies directly opposite facing south.

The largest stone of Castlerigg stands beside a unique rectangular enclosure, built within the ring but with the circle stones forming its fourth side. It seems to be contemporary with the circle, although its function remains unclear. When it was excavated in the last century a deep pit filled with charcoal was discovered inside it. Several circular cairns were a later addition and their shapes can just be made out in the grass. In the distance, directly behind the major stone, Helvellyn peers over the shoulder of Lower Man, and looks down upon the circle.

An outlying stone, no longer in its original position, sits almost unnoticed beside the wall, near the corner of the field. Plough marks on

'The outlying stone, no longer in its original position, sits almost unnoticed beside the wall, near the corner of the field.'

its front indicate it must have been buried before being re-erected in its present site. Beyond it, in the next field, once stood another stone circle, but sadly nothing of this remains.

Leaving the stones it is best to retrace your steps back down the lane for a hundred metres to where a footpath leads away towards the house at Nest. From there, after briefly rejoining the main road, a path cuts away down the hill and back to Dale Bottom.

Castlerigg is a magical place, ringed by high mountains in all directions. In the quiet of the evening or early morning it has an atmosphere which can be almost overwhelming. Stand alone, within the stones, and look around. You seem to be standing, at the very centre of everything.

2. Bampton Common

Approx. distance: 8 miles

Approx. time: 5 hours

Starting point: Bampton G.R.515183

O.S. Outdoor Leisure Sheet: 5

Grid references: cairn G.R.492164; standing stones G.R.491163; Towtop Kirk G.R.493179; cairn G.R.499195

In the quiet of the eastern Lake District, Bampton and Bampton Grange eye each other sleepily across the River Lowther. To the east is the limestone scar of Knipe Moor, while to the west the first low hills rise up towards the distant High Street range.

Just up a short side valley from Bampton is the great dam which holds back the waters of Haweswater Reservoir. Above the lake is Bampton Common, a beautiful, little-visited landscape of high fells and hidden valleys where even the golden eagle can still be seen quartering the empty hillsides.

As you leave the village, and just before the tiny school is reached, a footpath leads off to the right, up and across the fields. In early summer these are beautiful hay meadows, knee-deep in buttercups and clover. Beyond the first fields is an area of scattered, mature oak woodland, rich in birdlife and wild flowers. Through the trees, the reed-fringed Littlewater Tarn fleetingly appears below, beside the farm of the same name.

After briefly rejoining the lane, the path climbs up again across the high fields, between scattered rocky outcrops, to the farm buildings at Drybarrows. Just beyond the farm the moorland proper begins, and a path leads away due south to skirt around the hill called Pinnacle Howe. In front, a large erratic boulder perches precariously on the hillside, and as the path turns back westwards, it is worth scrambling up to admire it. From the hilltop just beyond the view is magnificent. The whole of Haweswater opens up beneath you, and at the far end, the ridges of High Street climb steeply from the lakeshore and rise into the blue distance. A person standing in the same spot in Neolithic times would have seen a very different landscape. The reservoir would not

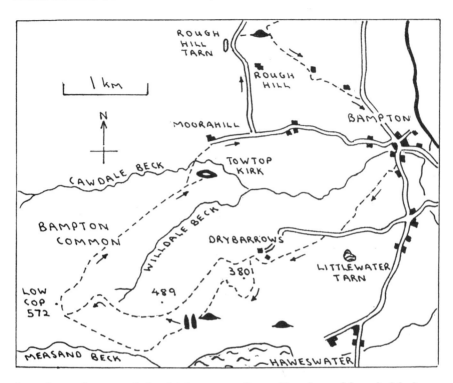

have been there, and the thick carpet of woodland would probably have been patched with the clearings of the first farmers to settle in the valley.

The path continues over a flat, marshy area, rich in bog plants and tiny sundews, and around Little Birkhouse Hill until a large burial cairn comes into view. It has been hollowed out and corrupted into a wind shelter, but it remains impressive, sited as it is in a narrow defile between the main hill and the smaller Four Stones Hill.

Just beyond, is a tiny rock-fringed tarn in the slightest hollow on the col, scarcely more than a permanent puddle, and a few metres further on two standing stones appear. The gap between them aligns perfectly with the cairn, which is just hidden over the low shoulder of the hill. Were these the entrance stones to a sacred area around the cairn? Were they the dividing line between this world and the world of the dead? Does the name of the hill indicate two other stones, possibly at the other end of the narrow pass? The place is atmospheric, and retains a peaceful timelessness, undiminished by the passing millennia.

'Were they the dividing line between this world and the world of the dead?'

Beyond the stones, the track drops down into Fordingdale Bottom, but our route climbs up through the ferns to reach the higher path. Larksong seems to fill the air, and wheatears stand watchful on the scattered rocks as the view widens and the track winds its way upwards towards Low Kop. In ancient times, this route would almost certainly have continued up the ridge to join an important trackway which crossed the hills and linked the two important Neolithic settlement areas of southern and north-eastern Lakeland. The track across Bampton Common would have been a spur leading off towards the settlements near Shap. At almost 2000 feet it seems no more than a gentle stroll up onto the main ridge away to the west, but here we must turn our backs on the high hills and drop pleasantly down the long ridge of the Hawse.

At the foot of the ridge is an area of level moorland enclosed on three sides by Cawdale Beck and its smaller tributary, Willdale Beck. Close to the steep bluffs above the river are the strange earthworks of Towtop Kirk. A low, circular, stone bank surrounds a jumble of stones and larger blocks, overgrown with nettles and reeds. This ancient henge is slightly smaller but similar in scale to King Arthur's Table at Penrith, but it seems to lack the interior ditch. The blocks in the centre are probably the remnants of a cairn, but too little remains to be certain. Like so many pagan monuments, its name was an attempt to Christianise the site in more recent times but, like Sunkenkirk, its ancient origins are not so easily disguised.

The path crosses the beck at a beautiful ford. The water is fast and clear and clumps of water crowsfoot with its white flowers wave gracefully in the shallows. It may be necessary to wade the stream, like the visitors to Towtop probably did five thousand years ago, but the stony bottom is smooth and the water pleasant on a warm day.

From the ford, the lane at Moorahill Farm is quickly reached and followed, turning north to Rough Hill and on to Rough Hill Tarn. Striking out eastwards across the edge of the moor, an overgrown cairn can be

Rough Hill cairn with Cross Fell beyond.

found just before the wall is reached. Much of its stone has been removed, and the nearby wall probably built with it. The large base stones could well be the kerbstones of the cairn. Despite this, it is a peaceful site and the view away to the east, to distant Cross Fell, makes it worth the visit.

From the cairn a path leads to a bridleway, past Gillhead and Woodfoot, to reach the road at Toddle Cottage which quickly takes you back into Bampton.

This is not a walk of spectacular monuments, of great circles and mighty stones, for the sites are small and secretive. But this is a sacred area. Many of the local names such as Hullockhowe, Drybarrows and The Howes hint at other burial cairns and mounds long gone. Pass between the standing stones on Bampton Common and you enter an area that would once have been hallowed ground. Fortunately for us, it has remained largely undisturbed and unaltered, and it is still possible to experience a landscape that our ancient ancestors would find almost familiar.

3. Loadpot Hill

Approx. distance: 11 miles

Approx. time: 6 hours

Starting point: Howtown G.R.443197

O.S. Outdoor Leisure sheet: 5

Grid references: The Cockpit G.R.482222; stone circle G.R.457194; Lambert Lad stone G.R.458188; ancient yew G.R.434184

Howtown is a small hamlet on the quiet eastern shore of Ullswater. The walk starts up the tiny lane beside the hotel, passes the house at Mellguards and follows the well-marked path out onto the open fellside. It gradually climbs, with the wooded slopes below falling away to the lakeshore, while the craggy hillside of Swarth Fell rises steeply above.

After a while, the well-trodden track crosses Swarthbeck Gill which tumbles out of a steep and wooded gully in Raven Crag. Beyond Auterstone Wood it becomes gradually steeper, climbing across the hillside to Barton Park Wood, crosses Aik Beck, and levels out onto the open moor.

Before long, and just after the next stream, the low stones of The Cockpit come into view. This circle, built into a raised bank comprises many small stones, a lot of which have fallen, but it is an atmospheric place, and in the distance Blencathra watches broodingly over the lower hills.

It is still a meeting point for many paths, and would have been so when it was first raised in the Bronze Age. The main trackway from south Lakeland to the Penrith area, passing over High Street, would have been crossed at this point by another leading from Castlerigg to Shap, and it is no surprise that such an important crossroads would have been marked in some way.

Our walk follows the first of these tracks, also taken by the much later Roman road, back to the south-west into the high hills towards High Street. After returning a short way along the approach route, a small cairn marks the point where the ancient route leads up the gentle slopes of Barton Fell. It is a pleasant grassy path which winds easily

The Cockpit

uphill, across wild and featureless moorland, until it levels off and a boundary stone is reached.

This is the first of many which mark the route, quite probably as it would have been marked thousands of years ago. After a second stone, a shallow valley opens up to the right and in it, just above the marshy stream bed, is the ruins of another small stone circle.

It is not easy to spot from the path and is little visited, but it can be located as it is in the only patch of short green grass in the valley. Above it the squat bulk of Loadpot Hill rises above the head of the stream.

It is a puzzling site, with only half the circle left and the stones seemingly too crowded together. It is almost as if the missing stones were uprooted and added to the remaining half at some point in its history. To add to the confusion, all the stones have fallen, resulting in a jumbled semi-circle of the shapely blade-like slabs.

Returning to the route another boundary stone is soon reached in a small rocky gully beside the path. This one is different from all the others. Named on the map as the Lambert Lad, it is an ancient stone, not propped up as the others are by many smaller stones, but deeply embedded in a socket in the ground and well weathered. It certainly predates the others, and is in all probability an original stone marking

The ruined circle of Loadpot Hill

the route over the hills. It also marks the source of Swarth Beck which flows down beside the circle and could have been a place of some significance in ancient times.

From here the old trackway seems to contour around the top of Loadpot Hill, but the modern path climbs up and over its summit. It is well worth the climb, if only for the enormity of the view which opens up in all directions from the plateau.

To the west, the high ridges of Helvellyn and Blencathra dominate the scene and to the south the broad shoulders of High Street block the horizon. Away eastwards, Cross Fell rises clear above the Eden Valley while the far off hills of the Yorkshire Dales appear almost cloud-like and ethereal at the very edge of the sky.

After dropping down from the top, past a small ruined building and another marker stone, the path soon begins to climb again towards Wether Hill. Here we must leave the old trackway as it continues over High Street, down past Troutbeck and on towards the settlements of

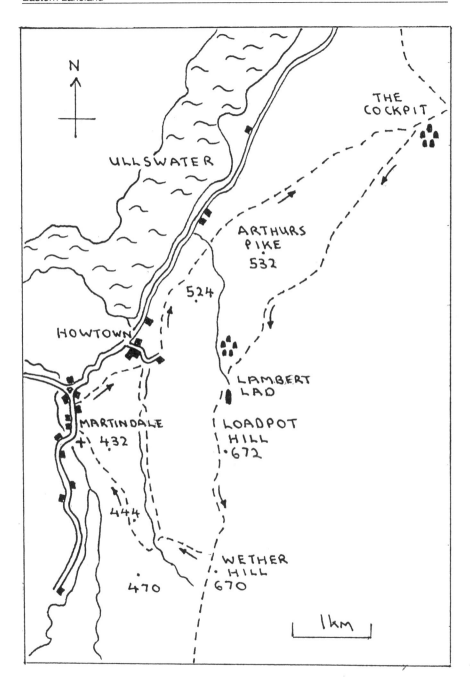

southern Lakeland. The path which is marked on the map dropping off to the right, seems not to exist on the ground, so instead carry on until a small cairn is reached and descend the easy grassy slopes from there, down to the ruined buildings beside the stream. If you are lucky, you might see the small wild herd of jet black ponies which graze these otherwise empty fells.

After crossing stepping stones over the infant Fusedale Beck, a good path climbs up onto the fine rocky ridge of Brownthwaite Crag. This is a superb viewpoint looking along the whole length of Bannerdale from High Street all the way down to the lakeshore. It is tempting from this point to scramble up to the rocky narrow summit of Pikeawassa just ahead for an even better view, before returning to the path. From the col, it traverses down into the valley, above the trees, to reach the tiny lane beside the Old Church of St. Martin.

A church has stood on this site for 750 years, although the present building dates only from Elizabethan times, and in the churchyard stands one of the oldest trees in England. This old yew is at least 1300 years old and probably older, and would have been a place of pagan worship long before the early Christians built the first church beside it. Its hollow and divided trunk, gnarled and knotted, sprouts branches which hang all the way to the ground, from where new and vigorous growths have sprung, forming a magnificent canopy of green.

It was probable that these trees were worshipped because of their great longevity and yet their counter association with death from their poisonous berries. It was thought that anything which so encompassed life and death must be a symbol of the gods. These tree cults most likely date back to Neolithic times, and so our ancient ancestors could well have passed just such a tree as this, and added another shiny stone or coloured ribbon to its many tokens and decorations.

Passing by it today, it is but a short walk back down the road before a path to the right skirts the lower slopes of Steel Knotts and drops back down to Howtown.

This is a big walk over big hills, across wild featureless moors and windswept ridges. The mountains and the views have remained largely unaltered, except that in places, it is probably more remote from civilization now than it would have been four or even five thousand years ago.

4. Askham Fell

Approx. distance: 7 miles

Approx. time: 4 hours

Starting point: Askham G.R. 513238

O.S. Outdoor Leisure Sheet: 5

Grid references: Tumulus G.R.494229; The Cockpit G.R.483223; White Raise cairn G.R.488224; cairn circle G.R.494219; Cop Stone G.R.496217

The village of Askham, with its sloping green and its terraces of old stone cottages, sits at the foot of a vast tract of moorland spreading away to the south-west, climbing up to the mountains of the High Street range. Known as Askham Fell it is covered in sites and monuments of the Bronze Age people who must have lived and farmed on this high plateau.

Leaving the village the road to the west becomes a lane, then a track and finally a path leading through the parkland of the Lowther Estate. Just as the moorland proper is reached, a strange site can be seen to the north of the path in front of the woodland on Skirsgill Hill. Marked on the map as a settlement, it is a strange jumble of stones and banks and ditches forming no apparent coherent shapes or patterns.

Passing beyond this on to the open fell, the low mound of a tumulus is soon reached. It is mostly grassed over, but several large rocks protrude at its top. Just beyond it a large limestone slab seems to have some smaller stones built against it. This could possibly be the remains of a kist, from which the mound has long since been removed.

Skirting around the hillside below Heughscar Hill, the old Roman road, known as the High Street, is soon reached, which leads you directly to the strangely named Cockpit. It cannot be a coincidence that so many of the Roman roads lead straight through or past ancient monuments. Perhaps the invaders needed to show their dominance over the old powers and religions.

The Cockpit is a Bronze Age stone circle, about twenty-five metres across, of low stones, many of which have now fallen. It is built into a low bank and appears to have the remains of a cairn just inside its north-western arc. Several stones have been moved or rolled out of place over the years, but the circle retains its integrity.

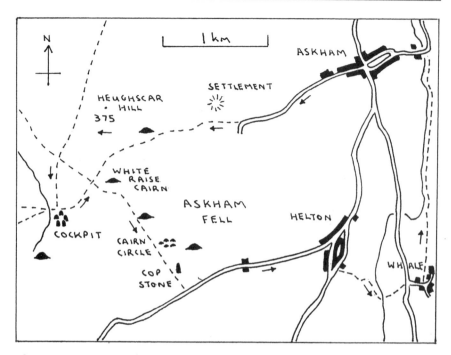

This was an important place, as it was here that two of the main trading routes of the district crossed. The track from Long Meg and her Daughters and the great henge at Mayburgh passed here before climbing up over Loadpot Hill and on towards the southern lakes. The other, from the settlements at Shap travelled westwards heading towards Castlerigg. It is quite possible that the stone axes from the axe factory at the Langdale Pikes would have been brought this way to be bartered or sold at the great northern circles. It is still the focal point of the moor nowadays and is well visited by walkers who sit on its stones and admire the view.

Above the circle to the south-west, a boundary stone is visible on a low bluff above the headwaters of the stream which passes close by. The water-worn grooves in its top suggest it has been in an upright position for hundreds, if not thousands of years, and may well have originated in one of the moorland's ancient circles.

Many stone cairns can be seen dotted across the moor but most are probably the result of land clearance in ancient times rather than for burials. However, the large tumulus of White Raise has a stone kist still clearly visible at its centre and the remains of a broken limestone cap-

'At the meeting of four trackways, the Cockpit is the focal point of the moor, and is well visited by walkers who sit on its stones and admire the view.'

ping stone. This mound is on high ground and is a prominent feature with the moor sloping away to either side.

Following the track south-east from here, a very strange cairn is soon reached. Appearing to be little more than a rocky outcrop festooned with reeds, it is in fact a tiny ring cairn with a narrow entrance leading into an open space with kerb stones lining the inner wall. It is very similar in structure to one on Eyam Moor in Derbyshire, with the largest stones framing the gap in the ring. Now rather sad and neglected, it sits unnoticed and overgrown beside the path.

Several hundred metres further on is a much more recognizable monument, a cairn circle with huge outward-leaning kerb stones jutting from a low stony bank. Built on a slight rise in the landscape, it resembles a crown with taller stones alternating with lower ones. The size of the kerb stones is unusual, especially for such a relatively small

'Several hundred metres further on is a cairn circle, with huge outward-leaning kerb stones jutting from a low stony bank.'

cairn and, despite the loss of most of the cairn material, it remains an impressive and powerful monument.

Beyond the cairn circle another tumulus can be seen, and on the near horizon a single standing stone beckons. It is known as the Cop Stone, and is in fact the last remnant of a stone circle, because the line of a raised circular bank can still be made out beneath the heather and grass. The stone is large and imposing and points powerfully up into the sky as a last reminder of the great monument that once stood here.

The path now drops down to a moorland road which leads down to the quiet little village of Helton. From here the road can be followed back to Askham but a more pleasant route is to take the old bridleway down to where a footbridge crosses over the River Lowther. The trail leads on into the tiny hamlet of Whale, where a path can be taken through a beech plantation carpeted in celandines in the spring to rejoin the river. From there it is a pleasant stroll back to Askham with

'The Cop Stone is large, and points powerfully up into the sky as a last reminder of the great monument which must once have stood here.'

the river on one side and the rocks of Burtree Scar above you on the other. Magnificent beech trees, in which red squirrels are still common, line the track and make a fitting end to such a fine walk.

Askham Fell is a jewel amongst moorlands, rich in evidence that our people once lived and worked up on this high plateau. No one lives up there now, and only the skylarks protest as you walk this ancient landscape of our ancestors.

5. Mayburgh Henge

Approx. distance: 4 miles

Approx. time: 2 hours 30 mins.

Starting point: Eamont Bridge G.R.523288

O.S. Outdoor Leisure sheet: 5

Grid references: Brocavum Roman Fort G.R.538289; King Arthur's Round Table henge G.R.523283; Mayburgh henge G.R.519284

The great henge of Mayburgh stands on a narrow neck of raised land between the rivers Lowther and Eamont, before they meet two miles further downstream at Brougham. It would have been here that the pre-historic track from Morecambe Bay dropped down from the mountains and crossed the River Eamont before turning north for Long Meg and on to Scotland.

There is no evidence that the site was chosen for defensive reasons, and it is more likely that the joining together of the two rivers held a more spiritual or religious significance. Interestingly, the small henge at Towtop Kirk on Bampton Common is also sited at the confluence of two rivers. What is certain is that the area has been of importance for at least four thousand years, and a major crossing point of the river for probably even longer.

Our walk follows the River Eamont to where it joins with the Low-ther, and then back along an old Roman road to the henge. Starting at Eamont Bridge, a track runs beside the river to a modern house on the site of an old mill. Here a path bends through a small patch of scrubby woodland, giving some idea of what the whole area must once have looked like.

Beyond the trees the footpath follows the riverside, past a number of weirs, along banks lined with magnificent old ash trees, including one ancient specimen with a completely hollow trunk. Black-headed gulls wheel raucously in the air, mallards are everywhere and a pair of goosanders shelter from the fast-flowing current in a quiet eddy against the far bank. Beyond the river, old river channels show how the course of the rivers must have changed many times over the years, but several areas of wooded high ground must always have stood above the waters.

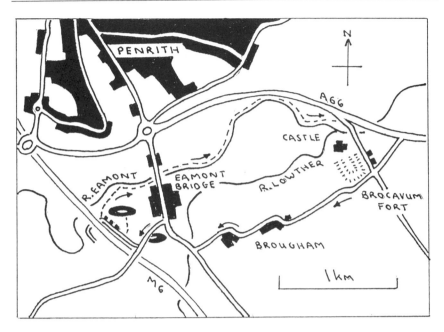

The river meanders close to the main road before looping away again to join with the Lowther below the spectacular ruins of the Medieval Brougham Castle. The path leaves the riverbank and crosses a field to a lane which leads back over a bridge to its entrance.

This was the place that the Romans chose to build their bridge, where roads from the coast and York met to cross the river before heading for the fortress at Carlisle. Behind the castle is the site of a large Roman encampment, still clearly visible in the field. It is called Brocavum, using an older Celtic name meaning the 'home of the badgers.' A wide ditch encloses a large rectangular area with a double bank inside. The ditch is deep and still holds water, and the banks are made of rough blocks of local red sandstone, now almost completely grassed over. The northern end of the camp was destroyed when the Medieval castle was built above the river, again to defend the crossing from the wilder tribes to the north.

When the Romans came was there still a community living there, dating back to when the great henge was built, or had it already been long abandoned and deserted? It must be remembered that the henge would have been at least as old to the Romans as the Romans are to us.

Our walk continues along the quiet lane following the line of the secondary Roman road from the camp to the west, eventually climbing over High Street and on towards the coast. It runs along the top of the bluffs above the river, past Brougham Hall, to the main road. After crossing the bridge over the Lowther, the henge of King Arthur's Round Table is soon reached.

This is a classic henge, with a high outer bank surrounding an interior ditch and enclosing a levelled area about fifty paces across. Within it is a central raised platform, although it is doubtful if this is an original feature. The henge has a large entrance facing south-east, and there was once another to the north-west which was destroyed when the road was built. Two large standing stones also stood outside the entrance but these too, sadly, have long gone. The bank is still high, and like other henges, must once have sheltered the rituals and ceremonies from anyone outside.

Returning to the lane, the great henge of Mayburgh can be seen over to the west, and its huge central standing stone is clearly visible through the entrance, which faces towards the smaller henge. Follow the lane along to where a track leads off to the right, beside an enormous, but recently quarried stone, down to a stile giving access to the henge. The motorway runs right beside this track, but fortunately it is down in a cutting and has little visual impact although the monotonous roar of the traffic is only partly dulled by the screening trees.

'In the centre is a single standing stone, almost two metres tall, and weighing many tons.'

From outside, the henge appears too large to be man-made. The huge bank, up to ten metres high, is at least forty paces broad at its base, and is surmounted by tall oak and ash trees. From the rim, the huge circular amphitheatre is massively impressive. Built up of large water-smoothed rocks from the river, the banks surround a levelled space over a hundred paces across. In the centre is a single standing stone, almost two metres tall, and weighing many tons. It was once in a setting of four stones, and four more flanked the entrance to the south-east, although all but this remaining giant have now gone.

This must have been a massive undertaking. Easily the largest pre-historic monument in northern England, thousands of tons of stone were moved from the riverbed to raise the banks. It must have needed a sizeable community to construct it, and this indicates a large residential population living for at least part of year on the neck of land between the two rivers. It is probably older than the smaller henge at Arthur's Table, built before the large tribal groupings broke up in the later Bronze Age. This could make Penrith one of the oldest continually lived in settlements in the country.

Leaving Mayburgh behind, the lane is followed until a path crosses fields, in full view of its high banks, before dropping down to the river. It was probably around here that a ferry would have crossed over the Eamont, extending the ancient trackway from High Street to the north. A short lane leads back to Eamont Bridge.

Mayburgh is an awe-inspiring monument, and is a great testimony to the vision and organisation of our ancestors. Despite the proximity of the town and the motorway, it is surprisingly peaceful and atmospheric. The great banks still serve their original purpose, and four thousand years later they still keep out the outside world.

6. Long Meg and Her Daughters

Approx. distance: 7 miles

Approx. time: 3hours 30 mins

Starting point: Little Salkeld G.R.566362

O.S. Outdoor Leisure Sheet: 5

Grid references: Glassonby cairn circle G.R.573394; Little Meg G.R.577375; Long meg and Her Daughters G.R.571372

This walk, from the pleasant village of Little Salkeld in the Eden Valley, begins uninspiringly along a path beside the Settle to Carlisle railway line. But persevere, for it ends along the ancient processional trackway from the great burial chamber at Glassonby to one of the largest and oldest stone circles in Britain and the giant outlying monolith of Long Meg.

From the village, take the lane running west until the houses end and fork right to follow the railway line northwards. It is a pleasant enough walk above the deep, wooded cutting and the views across the lovely Eden Valley help the time to pass.

When the railway crosses the river over a viaduct, the path descends quickly, passed the ruins of the Long Meg mine, to meet the river at Force Mill, where the dramatic weirs and waterfalls quickly raise the spirit. For the next half mile the path winds through dense woodland, past some spectacular man-made caves, before breaking out into open pastureland and a pleasant stroll along the riverbank.

Before long a quiet lane is reached which is followed back eastwards towards Glassonby. After a short steep hill the first of the ancient sites can be found on a small rise in a field off to the left.

This is a large kerbed cairn, and enough remains to show its original size and importance in the ancient landscape. The kerb itself is over seventeen paces across and is round, but the cairn seems to extend northwards suggesting perhaps, that the kerb cairn was built onto an earlier Neolithic longcairn running north to south.

The two largest stones of the kerb could have framed an entrance also facing due south pointing directly towards the circle at Long Meg a mile and a half away to the south. It is possible that a processional avenue led between the two sites. It would have been used for the great ceremonies of life and death, with bodies taken from the circle to be

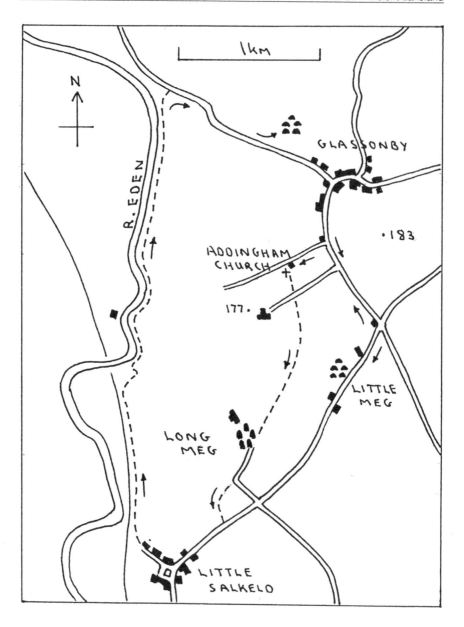

interred at Glassonby and bones of ancestors paraded back for festivals marking important events or significant dates in the calendar.

A similar avenue existed near Shap, between the Kemp Howe circle and the Hill of Skulls. This was lined with stones along its length and it is quite possible that here too, a stone-lined trackway once existed.

Unfortunately the avenue cannot be followed initially and our walk takes the lane through the village of Glassonby to where a tiny lane leads towards the old church of Addingham. Here another diversion can be taken, following the road for another half mile to visit the small cairn circle of Little Meg.

Tucked away at the edge of a field and sadly rather overgrown and neglected, this tiny ring is famous for its spirals carved into a low slab next to the larg- est of the circle stones. They are not immedi- ately obvious, but if you have the time, be patient, for in late afternoon sunlight they appear as if by magic in answer to the sun god for whom they were carved. The two spirals merge and intertwine and look like two eyes. Similar motifs have been found throughout the British Isles but rarely on such a small circle as Little Meg.

To regain the route of the processional avenue it is necessary to retrace the route to Addingham Church. Its position is significant, for many early Christian churches were built on more ancient pagan sites and this one lies away from the village exactly half way along the trackway between Long Meg and the burial cairn.

Although this church was only built in the 13th Century, a wheel-headed Celtic cross pre- dates it and could have been placed at this spot to show the pre-eminence of

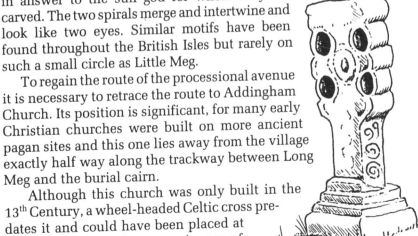

the new religion. Interestingly, and rather surprisingly, carved on the sides of the cross are more pagan intertwined spirals. Perhaps the people of the time were still hedging their bets and trying to appease the old gods as well as the new one.

From the church, a path leads through the churchyard and across a field to the top of a gentle rise which marks the high point of the ancient trackway. From this point the great ring of Long Meg and her Daughters comes into view and can be seen along the remainder of the approach which curves gently along the crest of the ridge.

As the circle approaches, its awe-inspiring size becomes more apparent, as it would have to the pilgrims of 5,000 years ago. The great stone of Long Meg itself dominates the ring and stands up above the skyline. In the last field before it is reached, two large stones, one in a wall and one beside a gnarled old ash tree, align perfectly with the line of the track and could just be the last remnants of the stone-lined avenue. From the nearer one the tip of Long Meg can just be seen over the low rise between them.

It is not until you reach the circle itself that the size of the stones can be fully appreciated. Some are almost Avebury-like in scale, and must weigh many tons each. There are over seventy of them remaining, all made of granite, some fallen, but many still standing in a flattened ring over a hundred metres across.

The circle, on its gently sloping site, is bisected by a farm road and has two huge ash trees within it, but it is the stones which dominate the scene. Two enormous blocks face each other from the east and west extremes of the circumference, and a wide entrance at the south-east is formed by four equally massive boulders.

Beyond the circle is Long Meg itself, a huge, red sandstone pillar over four metres high tapering from the base and notched at the top. On

the face nearest the ring are several clear carvings, concentric rings and again the spirals. If they were carved when the stone was first erected, probably a thousand years before those at Little Meg and some four thousand years before the Celtic cross in the churchyard, it indicates the great importance and longevity of the symbolism.

The positioning of Long Meg, some thirty metres outside the ring, was done intentionally and precisely. Seen from the centre of the circle, the sun on mid-winter's day sets into the notch at its top. Its height lifts it above the horizon, which probably explains why it is a tall sandstone finger instead of a lower, squatter granite boulder.

Leaving the circle, a short lane and farm track take you back to the road which drops quickly back into Little Salkeld.

In Neolithic times, Long Meg and her Daughters was a site of great importance, and five thousand years later it still has the power to make you catch your breath. To be able to approach it along the ridgeback, as the orig-inal worshippers must once have done, is both inspiring and humbling, and one not to be squan-dered by taking the car straight to it. Enjoy the pil-grimage, feel the history, for this really is an ancient walk.

'a huge red sandstone pillar tapering from the base and notched at the top.' /

7. Knipescar Common

Approx. distance: 4 miles

Approx. time: 2 hours

Starting point: Bampton Grange G.R.522181

O.S. Outdoor Leisure sheet: 5

Grid references: Knipescar stone circle G.R.528193

This is definitely a walk for the enthusiast. Knipescar stone circle is small and well hidden away amongst the limestone pavement and deep vegetation up on the high common, and it is a real challenge to find it. Knipe Moor itself, rises dramatically above the village of Bampton Grange and the valley of the River Lowther. The bracken-covered slopes steepen to a long limestone scar which rings the hillside, jutting out in the centre like the prow of a ship.

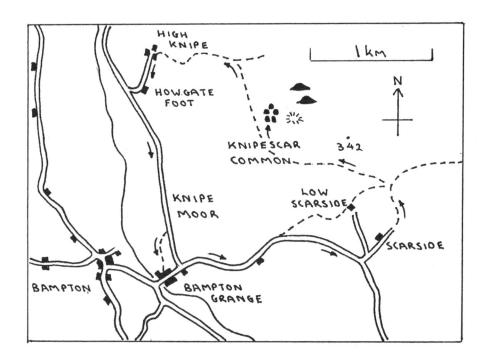

The route starts in the village by the old church and follows the road eastwards up the hill to the farmhouse at Scarside, where a good track leads up onto the open fellside. A footpath via Low Scarside is an alternative, but the path seems to disappear into impenetrable gorse high on the hillside.

The walk along the top edge is wonderful, crossing grassland speckled with wild flowers and butterflies, and winding through thickets of gorse marvellously carved by the nibbling teeth of the sheep. Mountain hares seem to be everywhere and often almost explode from beneath your feet and clatter off into the undergrowth. As the path climbs, patches of bare limestone pavement appear and the dip slope of the scar becomes covered in a sea of bracken.

It is very difficult to visualize how the moor would have looked 4000 years ago. The dense belt of woodland dividing the plateau would not have been there, giving it a much more open aspect, as the original tree cover would have been much lighter and largely cleared during the previous thousand years. Similarly, the thick carpet of bracken would not have existed. This plant tends to colonize areas which have been disturbed, often when the natural cover of heather and grass has been burnt off to improve the grazing.

The circle is hidden away to right of the track, close to the belt of woodland, marked only by a wooden post which just stands above the ferns.

All that remains is a low bank about sixteen paces across with many large pieces of limestone which have toppled and broken. An unusual feature is a large central slab which has been fantastically weathered and carved by the elements. It is quite probable that the circle has not been destroyed by man but has simply suffered at the hands of the weather as the limestone has gradually dissolved over the years. Other limestone circles, like the one in the great henge at Arbor Low in the Peak District, have suffered a similar fate.

Beyond the belt of trees lie several tumuli and an ancient enclosure, but unfortunately they are not accessible from the circle. They do indicate, however, that the common was a site of some importance in the Bronze Age.

In the summer, this is a claustrophobic place with the encroaching ferns towering over the low stones, but try to picture it as it must once have been.

The circle, with its large central slab would have stood beside a track

'An unusual feature is a large central slab which has been fantastically weathered and carved by the elements.'

which would have crossed the moor, running from the great circles and avenues near Shap, northwards towards Mayburgh henge at Penrith. Travellers would have passed between the two important settlement areas perhaps to trade in tools or ornaments or jewellery. Perhaps it was along this very route that the first artisans skilled in metalwork travelled up from the south to show their wares. Beyond the small ring, several large burial cairns would have been clearly visible with a cluster of circular huts sheltering in the slight dip between. Perhaps the circle was for the use of the people who lived up there, or perhaps travellers would have stopped as they crossed the high moor.

The ancient track continues across the moor, following the line of the edge until a shelterbelt of trees is reached, and then turns down the hill to High Knipe. From there, a lane leads down to Howgate Foot and to the moorland road which crosses the lower slopes. Soon after it leaves the moor behind, a path cuts across the fields and back into Bampton Grange.

Not a spectacular circle, but an interesting walk along the line of an ancient trackway with fine views away to the Lake District mountains in the west, and a real challenge. Not many people can say, 'I found the circle on Knipescar Common!'

8. Skellaw Hill

Approx. distance: 5 miles

Approx. time: 2 hours 30 mins

Starting point: Shap G.R.562153

O.S. Outdoor Leisure sheet: 5

Grid references: Hill of Skulls G.R.556155; Thunder stone G.R.552157; Goggleby stone G.R.559152; Kemp Howe stone circle G.R.567133

Skellaw Hill is a low rise in the land, above the River Lowther, just outside the town of Shap. On it once stood a huge burial chamber, known as the Hill of Skulls, linked by a sweeping avenue of stones to a great circle at Kemp Howe two miles to the south-east. Sadly, although it is a pleasant and interesting walk, it is also a testimony to the wanton destruction wrought upon our ancient heritage over the last three centuries.

For thousands of years it probably remained virtually intact, the still lingering memory and fear of the pagan gods protecting it. Then in the 18th century, as people became divorced from the past and the population grew, the destruction began.

All but the largest stones of the avenue were taken down and broken up for buildings and stone walls. Then the great Hill of Skulls was ploughed down to make a few extra rows of crops, and the huge stones of Kemp Howe rolled aside to make way for the new railway line. Finally, as if to add insult to injury, the enormous Hardendale Quarry works were built to tower over the old stones, which now sit in the nettles beneath its belching chimney stacks.

Despite all this, amazingly, enough survives to piece together the remaining clues to recreate something of this ancient landscape. The Goggleby Stone still sits on its low hill to mark the route of the avenue, and from the largest stone of Kemp Howe the Hill of Skulls can still be seen in the distance between the trees.

Start the walk from the centre of Shap by the small fire station where a side road and a back lane lead out to join the road going west towards Bampton. As the buildings are left behind, a path crosses the fields on the right to the Hill of Skulls. Now little more than a large hump in the field, it is still a commanding viewpoint and it is not difficult to imagine processions approaching up the hill towards it.

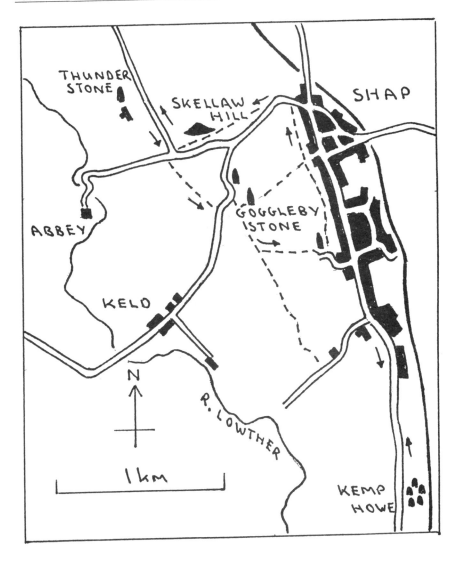

The path rejoins the road at the junction, and an interesting diversion is to follow the road north for a quarter of a mile to where a huge natural erratic known as the Thunder Stone can be seen in a field next to the farm. It is quite probable that this and several other nearby natural features were all important facets of the Neolithic complex.

From the Goggleby Stone, the Hill of Skulls is still clearly visible in the distance.

Returning to the junction, a narrow walled track lined with wild flowers leads to Keld Lane and the Goggleby Stone. This enormous stone stands about two metres high and is almost the shape of an axe head with the broad blade at the top, tapering towards the ground. Why it of all the stones survived we will never know but perhaps its sheer bulk prevented its destruction. It commands a gentle rise, and looking back, Skellaw Hill is still clearly in view. Another stone is directly aligned between the two, leaning precariously beside a wall in the shallow dip between them, marking the line of the avenue.

From the stone, the track south and a footpath across the fields brings you to yet another huge natural erratic, of similar size to the Thunder Stone and again almost certainly part of the ancient avenue. Several other large remnant stones can also be found in the many stone walls along the route. It is easy from here to return quickly back to Shap and end the walk, but for those brave enough to see it through, Kemp Howe is still another mile away to the south along the road.

The stones lie disconsolately beside the railway embankment, in the shadow of the works, overgrown and disregarded. The six, huge, egg-shaped, granite boulders are still impressive enough, however, to indicate that this must have been an imposing and important circle. It is so sad to see it in its present state.

This is not a walk of beauty on the high moors, nor an unspoilt and pristine landscape of ancient sites. It is a puzzle to be pieced together from the few remaining clues, and it is worthwhile for that. But don't go when the sun shines and the fells beckon. Go, instead, when swirling clouds hang low over the Lowther valley and the Goggleby Stone rises defiantly on its hill above the grey mists, and be grateful that enough has survived to allow us to rediscover the secrets of this once great complex of sites.

9. Crosby Ravensworth Fell

Approx. distance: 10 miles

Approx. time: 5 hours

Starting point: Crosby Ravensworth G.R.621147

O.S. Outdoor Leisure sheets: 5 and 19

Grid references: Castlehowe Scar stone circle G.R.587155; Iron Hill cairn circles G.R.597147; Oddendale stone circle G.R.592129; White Hag circle G.R.607116; longcairn G.R.615120

On these high moors and pasturelands on the eastern edge of Cumbria, lies the greatest concentration of ancient cairns and circles of anywhere in northern England. Possibly so much has survived because of the wildness of the landscape, but this was undoubtedly an important area in the late Neolithic and early Bronze Age.

The fell is a huge limestone plateau and the soil would have been light and easily worked, and the vegetation sparse and relatively easy to clear. Unfortunately, the limestone has also attracted the attention of modern man and the large Hardendale Quarry eats remorselessly into the western edge of the moor. Despite this, the walk has a feeling of remoteness and there are places on the fell where one can feel as removed from the 21st Century as anywhere in Lakeland.

Leave the quiet village of Crosby Ravensworth westwards on the high road to Shap, and either follow it to Castlehowe, or take one of the footpaths which run parallel to it. The site of an ancient settlement is marked by banks and a large boulder just to the right of the road. It is a quiet lane with wide views and you quickly arrive at the first circle at Castlehowe Scar. It is in a small field to the left, beside a stone wall just beyond the belt of woodland.

This tiny ring consists of ten stones of varying size, all of pink Shap granite. It also has one stone outside the ring and a small round one in the centre which may not be in its original position. It is possible that this is the remains of a kerbed cairn, although no cairn material survives, and some of the stones seem too large to be a kerb.

From the circle take the tiny lane running up onto the moor parallel to the trees, until a footpath leads you through the woods and out onto

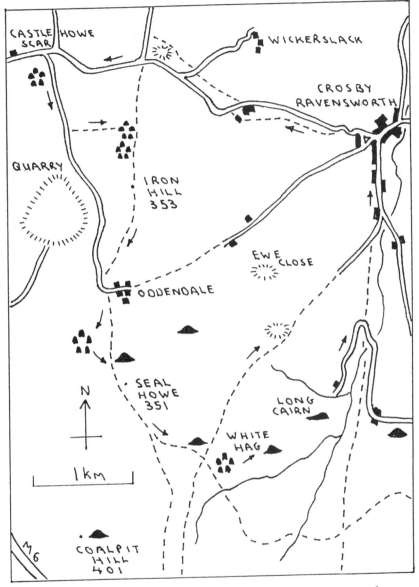

the open pasture land beyond. Iron Hill will now be in front and an easy walk will bring you to the top and two more circles.

The first, built into a wall, is definitely a kerbed cairn as part of the internal mound is still visible. The second and more interesting one is like Castlehowe, and has larger stones of pink granite but also three internal stones which could well be the remains of a burial cist. One of the nine circle stones has been displaced and is now outside the ring completely. If both are kerbed cairns the difference between them is both striking and puzzling.

The pair occupy a commanding height and the views are far reaching, from the High Street range to the west, to the north Pennines away to the east. Below is the enormous quarry which, surprisingly, is not too unattractive. The sculptured rock faces add a dramatic element to the more gentle scenery, and the tiny matchbox-sized vehicles are fascinating to watch from a distance.

From Iron Hill the route follows the ridge top along an old bridleway until it drops down to Oddendale, and a track leads up onto the open moorland of Seal Howe. Here the limestone breaks through the surface into wide pavements and the dark, protective cracks between the clints provide safe habitats for many small plants and animals. Delicate cranesbills and tiny ferns hide in the deep recesses and banded snails cluster together in the shade. Scattered across the limestone are many large blocks of granite, and one particularly large one leads the way towards the first true stone circle of the walk.

At first glance it appears to be a circle within a circle, but on closer inspection the inner one is again the kerb of a large cairn. The true outer circle is of twenty-eight granite stones in a ring twenty-eight paces across. The cairn ring is of smaller, almost touching stones, and is about seven paces across. It is quite possible that the cairn was constructed much later than the original circle. Inside are more scattered blocks including one of limestone. The two circles are almost exactly concentric and the pair must once have been a magnificent sight up on top of the open moor.

Looking back towards the track, a cairn can be seen beyond it on the slopes leading up to the top of the hill. It is made with large rough blocks of limestone and now has a modern cairn built onto it.

The track leads on over the hill and past several small plantations to where a path branches off to the left and rises up onto the outlying spur of Coalpit Hill.

As it climbs up it cuts through several limestone scars and at the top are some magnificent areas of pavement. This is a wonderful place, crossed by an old Roman road, and has one rather overgrown and hollowed-out cairn at the top. Two beautifully isolated trees crown the

The concentric rings of Oddendale stone circle.

hilltop and seem to sprout from the very rock itself. It is a perfect place to sit and rest and watch the buzzards spiralling up above the empty moors, their sharp cries mournfully breaking the silence.

As the path drops down the far side of the hill, away to the left is the tiny White Hag stone circle. Only five paces across, its eleven stones of pink granite sit in a wonderfully remote spot looking out over the Lyvennet Valley to the far Pennines.

From White Hag it is possible to return towards the hilltop and take

'White Hag stone circle above the Lyvennet valley'

the public bridleway all the way back to Crosby Ravensworth, passing the sites of several ancient settlements, at Ewe Locks and Ewe Close, en route. Alternatively, cross the White Hag pavement and follow the large wall. In the first field is a large well-preserved cairn of grassed-over limestone blocks still well over a metre high.

Further along, where the pastureland drops down towards the scattered woodland above the river, is a Neolithic longcairn. It is over thirty paces long, running from east to west and made from mostly granite boulders. It stands tall and its shape is clear, despite several old hawthorn trees growing from its ridge, and is one of the few good examples of a longcairn in Cumbria.

From the cairn, a track does lead past yet another settlement site and over the sometimes dry streambed and waterfalls of Bleabeck. It continues past the farmbuildings of Starleyford and to the public footpath which takes you back to the village. It should be noted, however, that no public right of way exists along this short section.

'where the pastureland drops down towards the scattered woodland above the river, is a Neolithic longcairn.'

Crosby Ravensworth fell is a wild and beautiful moorland, and, despite its proximity to the motorway and the quarry, it retains a remote air. It has a treasure chest of cairns and settlements and circles hidden away on its high limestone plateau, and no finer day can be had, away from the Lake District crowds, than exploring this ancient landscape.

10. Great Asby Scar

Approx. distance: 10 miles

Approx. time: 5 hours

Starting point: Orton G.R.623083

O.S. Outdoor Leisure sheet: 19

Grid references: Ring cairn and stone row G.R.647112; burial cairn G.R.648119; Hollin Stump cairn G.R.652116; Settlement G.R.673109; burial cairn G.R.653090; Gamelands stone circle G.R.640082

Orton village is only a few miles away from the M6, but it could be in another world. It is quiet and peaceful and the pace of life slows as the lanes narrow and the traffic noise fades into the distance. It sits in the valley below Great Asby Scar, a huge tilted plateau of limestone, which rears up above it like a breaking wave. There is plenty of evidence that our Bronze Age ancestors lived and died high up on its slopes, and at its foot a Neolithic stone circle, although battered and broken, has survived almost five thousand years of farming.

The walk starts in the village centre near the old church, where a lane leads past the vicarage, and a footpath towards Broadfell takes you out into the countryside. As soon as the houses are left behind, another track branches off to the right, over a small bridge and across the fields to the narrow lane near Scarside. Just past the farmhouse a path climbs up across the hillside towards the scar.

When the last of the stone walls is reached, the path comes to a crossroads and the left-hand track is taken up onto the crest of the hills. The remains of a small cairn lie near to the first band of exposed rock. Beyond, the path continues to a large wall with the open moor beyond. This is a bleak and featureless landscape which rolls away into the distance, and the paths across it are indistinct and often illusory. Far better to rely on the few distinct and reliable features for navigation, so after passing through the wall, follow it along on its western side.

The Thunder Stone is a large natural erratic boulder of pink granite built into the wall at the first bend. Just beyond it is an old quarry site and a large area enclosed by a high stone wall, and it becomes increasingly necessary to wind around or scramble over stretches of stone pavement. As the land begins to rise off to the left, several hundred metres away from the wall is the first important site on the walk.

Cresting a small, subsidiary hilltop is a large ringcairn of rough gritstone, which outcrops nearby above the limestone. It is about ten paces across and, most intriguingly, has a row of stones leading from it for almost a hundred paces towards the main hill beyond. There are also a number of small stones inside the ring, although whether they have simply rolled in or are the remains of an internal cairn is not clear.

This is a remote.and little visited site, unmarked on maps and away from all paths. Around it the moor sweeps away in all directions broken only by a single tree near the summit of the scar away to the south.

". . . a large ringcairn of rough gritstone . . . a remote and little visited site"

Follow the row of stones up to the top of the hill behind and down the other side, keeping in a straight line, and you come to two burial cairns just above a quiet hill road. The first is quite large and is made of limestone blocks with some larger pieces of granite, while the second has had most of its cairn material removed, leaving several of its kerb stones

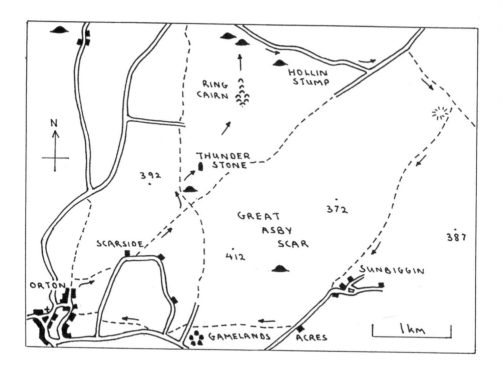

prominent. Is it just a coincidence that the stone row from the ringcairn points directly over the hill to the cairns or were the sites linked in some way?

Following the road eastwards towards the wall, another burial cairn known as the Hollin Stump can be seen in the first field on the right. This cairn is enormous, easily the largest remaining in Cumbria. It is all of twenty-three paces across, almost four metres high, and although wall builders have taken several large bites out of its perimeter, its scale is still quite breathtaking. A number of large kerb stones outside the cairn indicate that it must once have been even larger.

Was this the tomb of a great chieftain, or the communal burial place for the local community? Evidence from other large cairns would tend to indicate that it was raised for a single burial, but that further cremated remains could well have been added later. Close by is the quarry from where the stone for the mound was originally taken.

From the cairn the road is followed as it drops gradually down, through bands of exposed limestone, to where a track joins it from the right. This can be taken to shorten the route, as it leads pleasantly back through a narrow defile, across the top of the plateau, and down to the stone circle at Gamelands.

The longer walk continues down the road to a bridleway which follows the edge of the fields towards Asby Grange. Just over the crest of a low hill it turns right, back up onto the hillside. Here, beside the path, is the site of an ancient settlement. The walled banks and enclosures are still clearly visible, but they are confusing and it is difficult to see any cohesive pattern in them. Just below is a natural spring, and above, another small, ancient stone quarry.

From here the path climbs, and the true nature and extent of this wild and rugged plateau becomes obvious. Limestone pavements stretch away to the horizon, creating an almost lunar landscape. Tiny ferns hide in the dark recesses and the rock shimmers whitely in the summer heat. Groups of modern cairns and other weird rock structures just add to the strangeness of the scenery. Rabbits are everywhere, scuttling back to their burrows as you approach, and in the sky buzzards circle silently overhead.

The path reaches the crest of the ridge at a wall, and to the right of the track, where the wall surmounts a band of limestone blocks, is the most perfect place to sit and take in the whole scene. Asby Scar is like an island, surrounded by lowlands but with hills and mountains ringing the horizon in all directions. To the south the great northern ridges of the Howgill Fells stretch down to the River Lune, enclosing narrow shadowy valleys, while the ethereal outlines of the Pennines fade away into the distant east.

For those intrepid enough to try to reach it, another burial cairn sits on a small hilltop away to the west along the edge of the scarp. Again it is very large, built of limestone blocks, and once more, next to its own small quarry. Our route, however, drops down to the farm at Sunbiggin, along the lane to Acres, then across the fields to Knott Lane and the Gamelands stone circle.

This large ring of twenty-seven stones is in a field close to a wall. All but one are of pink granite and they form a rough circle forty-four paces across. One of the stones is beautifully crosshatched with veins of quartz crystals, giving it an almost unnatural appearance.

The two large gaps were probably made to allow the inside to be ploughed, and none of the stones now stand tall, but one can only

marvel at the sheer resilience of its survival down here among the fields. The size of its stones could well explain why it has escaped the destruction metered out to so many lowland rings.

Its position, directly below Knott Hill, the highest point of the scar, is no coincidence, for the hill and the circle are all part of the same ancient landscape. The stones pay homage to the 'mother mountain', and it, in its turn, towers protectively over the ring dominating the scene. It is also sited on the springline, near to where several clear streams emerge from beneath the limestone and begin their journey via the River Lune to the sea.

This combination of dominant hill and natural spring seems to have been one of great significance to the Neolithic people, and for the community living here this would have been seen as a site of great potency.

Even today, broken and bowed as it is, the circle retains a tangible aura of profound mysticism.

Great Asby Scar is a strange and atmospheric hill. It is an open and empty landscape of rock and moor that has altered little over the years, and its distant views and far horizons are almost as our forefathers would have seen them. This is a long walk, but one that is steeped in prehistory, one of those few remaining places where it is possible to look beyond the stones and still see the faint shadows of our remote past.

From the circle, paths and lanes lead directly back to Orton and the end of the walk.

11. The Tongue

Approx. distance: 8 miles

Approx. time: 4 hours

Starting point: Troutbeck G.R.407028

O.S. Outdoor Leisure Sheet: 7

Grid references: Cairns G.R.427028; Chambered cairn G.R.425076; Hird Wood circle G.R.416059

Troutbeck is a delightful old village which straggles along a narrow lane up on the hillside above the stream of the same name. Start near the centre and enjoy the walk past the stonewalled cottages and the three old roadside springs of St. John's, St. James' and Margaret's Wells, until the lane drops down steeply to the main road. Cross it and then turn back right and down through Town Head and out into the valley bottom along Ing Lane.

Ahead the two great valleys of Trout Beck and Hagg Gill are split by the shapely hill known as The Tongue. Beyond, Ill Bell with its cairned summit dominates the high outlying ridge of High Street.

Follow the lane over Ing Bridge and along pleasantly to Hagg Bridge, where the route turns up the hill to join a track leading from Troutbeck Park into the valley of Hagg Gill.

Unknowingly, we have been following the line of the old Roman road for some time, but from this point it begins to look like it did almost two thousand years ago. The lightly stoned track runs along a levelled course and meanders gently uphill above the stream, until it comes to a wide flat area below the steep slopes of the main ridge. Just to the left of the path are the remains of two burial cairns.

The first is about seven paces across and its bare stones are clearly visible from the path. The second is smaller, mostly grassed over and difficult to find, but interestingly a ring of kerb stones can still be seen surrounding it.

From here we leave the Roman road and climb up onto the long ridge of The Tongue, which stretches away to the south. After only a couple of hundred metres two more cairns appear. The nearest is large in area but barely visible above the vegetation, but the next is much more inter-

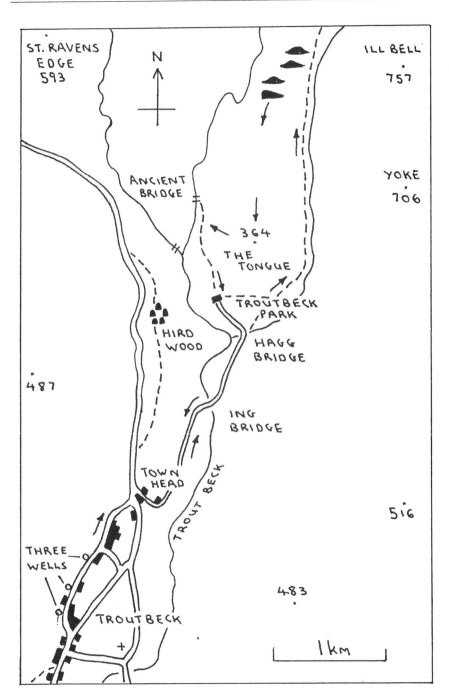

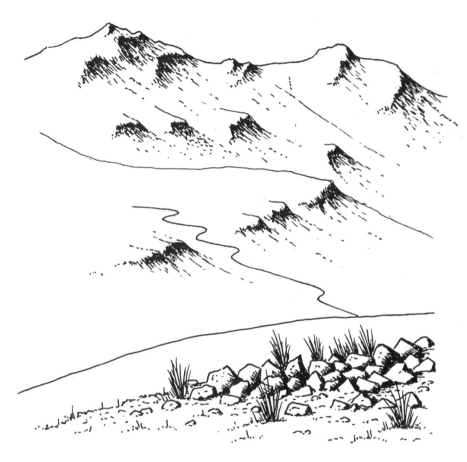

esting. What at first seems just a chaotic jumble of rocks is, quite possibly, the ruins of a Neolithic chambered longcairn.

The stones have been considerably rearranged and some now form a rough shelter, but two very large capstones lie amongst the smaller stones. One still stands upon low supporting stones, although whether this is its original position is doubtful. Nevertheless they indicate at least one chamber and possibly more. The outline of the cairn is difficult to make out but it does not appear to be circular, and with the bulk of the cairn material and the capstones being at one end, a longcairn seems most likely. It is in a wonderfully wild place, looking up towards the head of the valley at Threshthwaite Mouth.

The ridge rises gradually above the cairns and it is possible to follow a faint path between the rocky outcrops, along the crest, over a low fence and along to its highest point. It is not until the final few steps up to the cairned and pointed summit that the magnificent view to the south is revealed.

The valley runs straight as an arrow between high ridges to Windermere. There, framed by hills and speckled by wooded islands, the great lake reflects the midday sun perfectly. It is a wonderful place to sit and imagine the great forests, which would once have carpeted much of the lowland spread out below. Some fragments of the wild wood still cling, largely untouched, to the steeper slopes of the hillsides.

From the top, the route drops down westwards to join a path just to the south of a belt of such trees beside the river. The descent is steep but straightforward, although it is necessary to negotiate another low fence half way down.

Having reached the path, take it upstream for a short distance, through the woods and past the waterfalls to find a beautiful and ancient bridge over the river. Built of huge flat stones, it appears as old as the cairns on the hill above it, but even assuming it is in fact more recent, it is quite probably on the site of an ancient crossing leading from the cairns to a stone circle which is hidden away in the trees above.

Unfortunately it is no longer possible to reach the circle from here, so it is necessary to return down the path to Troutbeck Park. From there a lane leads back to Hagg Bridge and the route can be retraced to the village.

The circle in Hird Wood can be visited along another path leaving the main road several hundred metres out of Troutbeck, and it is a walk of about a mile. One prominent stone remains freestanding with three more incorporated into a wall. Others are fallen and scattered about making it very difficult to visualize its original shape, but it is possible that the large stone once stood in the centre of the circle.

This is a strange complex of sites, natural springs, burial cairns, a stone circle and an ancient river crossing. Is it possible that they were all linked together by a prehistoric trackway that once passed through here from the great settlement area of south Lakeland and the stone axe factory at Langdale? It would have kept to the high ground, passing the springs and the old circle, before crossing the river at the site of the old bridge, and climbing past the cairns and on into the mountains. Having crossed over the High Street range it would have eventually dropped down to Askham Moor and to the large settlements around modern Penrith and the great ring at Long Meg. The Romans simply followed part of the pre-existing track over the hills.

If this theory is correct, it clearly emphasises the complexity and interwoven nature of the society that existed before the Romans came. This walk merely takes another few pieces of the ancient jigsaw and drops them into place.

Western Lakeland

'Loft crag and its precipitous buttresses falling away into the valley.'

12. Langdale Pikes

Approx. distance: 5 miles

Approx. time: 4 hours

Starting point: New Dungeon Ghyll G.R.296064

O.S. Outdoor Leisure sheet: 6

Grid references: Thorn Crag site G.R.280070; Harrison Stickle G.R.281074; Loft Crag G.R.277072; Pike of Stickle G.R.274074; Mortcrag Moor site G.R.271081

The Langdale Pikes rise dramatically above the head of Great Langdale, their sharp volcanic spires dominating the valley. The highest point, Harrison Stickle, stands like a great cathedral above the lower crags and buttresses which are split by the deep chasms of Dungeon Ghyll and Stickle Ghyll.

It was here that Neolithic man discovered several outcrops of a hard volcanic rock which could be chipped and shaped to make sharp and durable blades. Of such quality were the tools and axes which they made here, that they have been discovered all over the British Isles, some beautifully polished and so cherished that they were buried beside their owners and within their most sacred monuments.

Waste chippings and discarded and broken blades can still be found at many sites, in the deep gullies and scree slopes below the cliffs and on the high plateau above them. Hand-sized rounded hammer stones, sometimes of a rock-type not found locally and which were used for knapping the axe stones, have also been discovered in some numbers. This walk visits a number of these sites which can still be explored and fascinating reminders of the past still discovered.

The walk begins beside the hotel and follows the left hand of three paths which climb the steep hillside. It initially takes a track which contours around the lower slopes towards the old hotel, before cutting up and across the tumbling waters of Dungeon Ghyll and climbing the slopes above to the first belt of cliffs. The path winds up a short scree-filled gully then contours around the hillside to the left to reach a wide, almost level area below the main crags of Harrison Stickle and Thorn Crag.

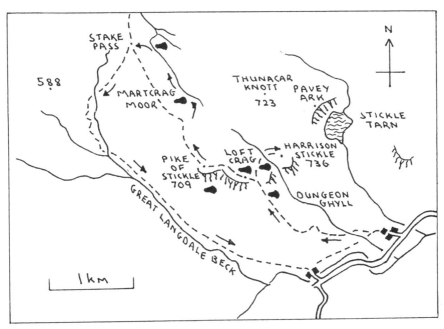

The deep chasm of Dungeon Ghyll itself slices through the cliffs, but our path takes the wide gently-sloping gully to the left. It is up here to the right of the path that many chippings and remnants of Stone Age tools have been found, and it is worth pausing and exploring the broken rocks below the crags.

At the top of the gully is a large plateau, above which rise the sharp summit cones of Harrison Stickle, Loft Crag and the Pike of Stickle. Follow the path to the right towards Harrison Stickle, and just before it crosses the stream which plunges into Dungeon Ghyll below, is an area of low rocky knolls. The ground here is littered with sharp-edged chippings and it is possible to see where the bedrock has been quarried and worked at.

Beyond the stream it is an easy scramble onto the rocky summit and a viewpoint almost unrivalled in the district. Below is Stickle Tarn, at the foot of the dark shadowy crags of Pavey Ark, and to the west the sharp tops of Pike of Stickle and Loft Crag. Behind them are arrayed the greatest peaks of Lakeland, the huge bulk of Bowfell, and beyond, Great Gable and the Scafells, ridge upon ridge fading into distance.

Having admired the view, it is necessary to retrace your steps back down to the stream, and over it to climb up to the lower but equally impressive summit of Loft Crag. This was another place where axes were made and many chippings can be found in the gullies and ledges leading to the cairn on its narrow ridge. It was here that I found a large stone which had been partly worked, with several flakes chipped away from one edge. It was simply lying in a pile of loose stones a short way below the summit.

It is a pleasant and easy scramble along an airy, rocky ridge to reach the Pike of Stickle, the steepest of the three pikes. The easiest route to its top is to traverse around to its further northern side where a break in the rocks allows an easy scramble to the top. Just below the cairn on the eastern side is a wide grassy ledge, where it is possible to shelter from the western wind and look back to Loft Crag and its precipitous buttresses falling away into the valley. It is below this spot that many of the best finds have been made in the gullies and scree slopes between the crags. Did our Neolithic ancestors sit here too, skilfully crafting blades which would be traded and treasured throughout the land, looking out at the scene of activity on the rock outcrops below?

After scrambling back down, a track leads northwards which can be followed for a short way before it is necessary to strike out across the rocky moorland to find the headwaters of Stake Beck. The tiny stream is followed as it twists and tumbles in its rocky bed down onto Martcrag Moor. This whole area has yielded many finds from Neolithic times, mainly waste chippings, although some hammer stones and broken tools have also been found. Most of the sites are now grassed over, but in several places the tiny stream has exposed areas of perfect stone flakes, as clean and unweathered as the day they were chipped from their core stones.

Partly worked stone from Loft Crag.

Stone chippings from Martcrag Moor.

Lower down, the stream levels out and more streamlets join it in a wide shallow basin. Our route leaves it here and climbs up over the moorland to the left to the top of Stake pass. This high point between the two streams of Stake Beck and Stake Gill is indicated by a cairn and a long finger of rock, now lying flat, but which probably once stood to mark the col.

From here the narrow path winds pleasantly downhill between hummocky glacial moraines until it crosses the widening stream over stepping stones and begins to drop down more steeply. It now becomes a well-constructed stone track which zig-zags down to the valley floor. The Pike of Stickle commands the skyline throughout the descent, constantly changing its shape as the path drops.

At an old sheepfold the beck is crossed again over a wooden footbridge and is then followed back towards the end of the lane coming up the dale. The ever-changing views of the Pikes above, the pollarded willows beside the river and a line of clearance cairns in the old fields all provide interest until the Old Dungeon Ghyll is reached. From there the road can be followed easily back to the start of the walk, or a footpath taken which crosses the lower slopes of the hillside to rejoin the path above the hotel.

This is a magnificent walk in spectacular surroundings, and it visits sites which were once of great importance to our Neolithic ancestors. To touch the very stones that they touched, and to search for tools and axes crafted by their own hands is fascinating. Let your imagination loose and you can get as close to ancient times here as it is possible to get anywhere in these islands.

13. Eskdale Moor

Approx. distance: 7 miles

Approx. time: 4 hours

Starting point: Boot, Eskdale G.R.173007

O.S. Outdoor Leisure Sheet: 6

Grid references: Brat's hill G.R.174024; White Moss East G.R.173025; White Moss West G.R.172024; Low Longrigg West G.R.171027; Low Longrigg East G.R.172028; Maiden Castle G.R.185054

Eskdale is a popular valley for tourists who flock there in summer to admire the scenery, but up on the moorlands to the north, little has changed for thousands of years. The evidence for a thriving Bronze Age community living and farming there is scattered across the moor, in one of the most dramatic natural amphitheatres in Britain.

Leaving the village of Boot and crossing the river, our route follows the upper of two bridleways steeply up onto the edge of Eskdale Moor. Several old peat cutter's huts mark the beginning of a large undulating plateau stretching away to the north and west. To the right of the path beside the huts is a small ring of stones, probably kerbstones from an ancient cairn. Many paths cross the moorland, but choosing one to take you to the first of the circles is not easy. It lies north-north-west from the stone huts, up on the central ridge of the plateau.

This first circle is known as Brat's Hill and is a fine ring of small stones about twenty-five paces across. Inside it are five well-preserved kerbed cairns, one of which has a large, but fallen, standing stone beside it. The circle sits below a large natural rock outcrop, which could well have been the original, religious focal point of the community in ancient times. Such features, called 'natural hill altars' by Julian Cope in his book 'The Modern Antiquarian', are found throughout the country and many circles and monuments are located close by them.

Just beyond it, are the paired White Moss circles, slightly smaller than Brat's Hill, and each with only one central cairn. The three rings are all in full view of each other, dominated by the steep rock outcrop, and together they make an impressive and atmospheric complex of sites, hidden away from the main paths across the moor.

The view from the stones is breathtaking, with Great Gable dominat-

The two largest stones of Whitemoss East, looking west towards Whin Rigg.

'The three rings are in full view of each other, and are dominated by the steep, natural rock outcrop.'

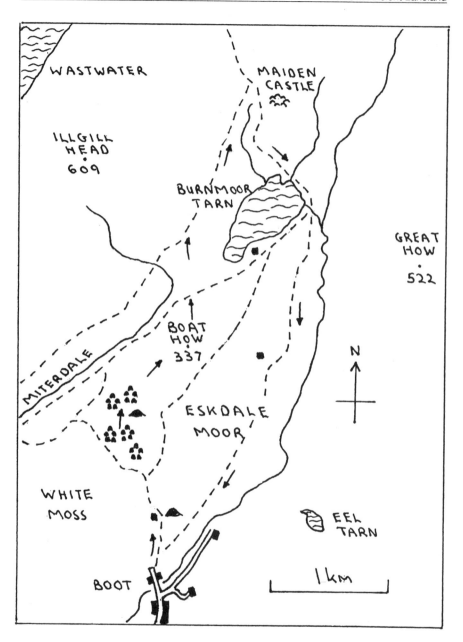

ing the distant skyline, while the huge bulk of Scafell rears up to the north-east.

To the west, the long high ridge of Illgill Head drops gradually down to the pass leading over towards Wastwater and Wasdale Head.

From White Moss strike out across the moor to the nearby ridge of Low Longrigg leading up to Boat Howe. The fells here are dotted with ancient cairns which are probably more the result of land clearance than places of burial. Low on the ridge are two more stone circles, similar in size to those at White Moss. Again both have a central burial cairn, and are also aligned south-west to north-east. The stones are small, but interestingly shaped, and the views towards Great Gable are magnificent.

The obvious question is: why are there five circles all sited so close together on Eskdale moor? All date from the Bronze Age, but does that

'The stones of Low Longrigg are small but interestingly shaped, and the view towards Great Gable is magnificent.'

mean that they were all in use at the same time? Were there days or nights when ceremonies, festivities or rituals were taking place in all the circles, and the moorland was thronged with people? The alternative would be that some circles replaced others as they fell into disrepair or out of favour. They certainly seem to have been in use for a considerable period of time because the internal cairns were probably added well after the circles were first built. And what of the 'Hill Altar'? Was it still an important part of the complex? Did it still have a role to play in the religion of the people of the day or was its importance just a distant folk memory from their primitive past?

All these questions are impossible to answer now, but it is fascinating to picture the wild moorland of today, alive with music and movement. The five circles all celebrating the rising of the sun, while on the great rock a High Priestess stood to welcome the first rays of light striking out from the horizon. Quite possibly the reality was much less dramatic but if Eskdale Moor can so inspire the imagination today, perhaps it also could all those thousands of years ago.

The route continues up the ridge to the summit of Boat How to admire the view, before dropping down into the valley to the north-west, above the waterfalls, and climbing up the lower slopes beyond to reach the main path coming up from Miterdale. Don't be tempted by the beautiful Burnmoor Tarn, because the moorland around it is wet and marshy in all but the driest conditions.

This path leads up to the pass down into Wasdale and just at the col, is Maiden Castle cairn. Perched on a gentle rise above the path, it is a large ringcairn with a large level clear space at its centre. Despite the fact that some of the stones have been rearranged to create a windbreak, it remains impressive and is in one of the most magnificent sites in the Lake District surrounded as it is by England's greatest mountains. Scafell, Great Gable, Kirkfell and Pillar all look down upon the cairn. Who could have chosen a more dramatic place for a burial site?

From Maiden Castle a good track skirts around the eastern edge of Burnmoor Tarn, and leads back across Eskdale Moor, before dropping down once more towards the village.

The moors above Boot are wild these days, but they were lived on and farmed thousands of years ago by a people who looked up at the same mountains, sat on the same rocks and drank from the same streams as we do today. If you ever feel the urge to get close to these ancient times then take a walk on Eskdale Moor.

14. Devoke Water

Approx distance: 3 miles

Approx. time: 2 hours (don't rush it!)

Starting point: High Ground, Birker Fell G.R. 171977

O.S. Outdoor Leisure sheet: 6

Grid references: Burial cairn G.R.152969; area of field cairns G.R.172977, 156974, 168977

Birker Fell is a great saucer-shaped basin of high moorland ringed by hills and crags. At its western end, Devoke Water fills a shallow hollow and spills over the rim into the steep sided gorge of Linbeck Gill. The centre of the basin is wet and beset with deep, uncrossable bogs and marshes, but on the freer draining slopes around its edges, a Bronze Age community once lived and farmed.

Our walk starts at the small moorland road which crosses the fell, near the isolated farmhouse of High Ground, where a track leads off towards Devoke Water. At the top of a gentle rise, the tarn suddenly comes into view and at its far end, on the low hills and framed against the sky, the remains of a great burial chamber can just be seen. It must have been sited so as to be visible from all directions, and must have been of great significance to the community to occupy such a position.

To reach it, the track continues below the cliffs of Seat Howe to the waters edge, and on to the old boathouse, where a path branches off towards the foot of the tarn. Several beautiful streams of crystal clear water bound down from the hillside, but some convenient stepping stones are sufficient to keep the feet dry. A tiny island in the tarn is a good indication of how the natural vegetation would develop if there were no grazing animals on the fells, for it is covered with a thick mat of birch, hawthorn and heather.

Thankful for the pleasant sheep-cropped turf and avoiding the wetter areas of the moor, the foot of the lake is soon reached with its great burial cairn on its prominent hill. Even in its present state it is visible for miles and must once have visually dominated the whole area. It is at least sixteen paces across and has larger kerb stones around its southern circumference. Sadly, much of the cairn material has been converted into a walkers' windbreak, but even this doesn't seem to detract from the magnificence of its position in the landscape.

Away to the west the sea shimmers in the afternoon sun and, to the east, the jagged tops of Rough Hill and Harter Fell rise up above the lower fells. Beyond, the great peaks of central Lakeland hunch up broodingly as the dark bruises of cloud shadows drift across the empty moorland.

Few places can be so easily accessible and yet have such a feeling of remoteness. It is a place to sit and rest, to let time pass by and picture the scene as it would have been thousands of years ago. It is little wonder it was chosen as the site for the great cairn.

The remains of the great burial cairn above Devoke Water.

The ground slopes away beyond the cairn to where Linbeck gill drops down into a steep and wooded gorge. It is best to cross it close to the tarn, where it is no more than a pleasantly tumbling stream, to avoid the scramble into its depths.

The whole of this area is a site of special scientific interest because of the bogs and marshes which lie in the hollows. The indistinct path

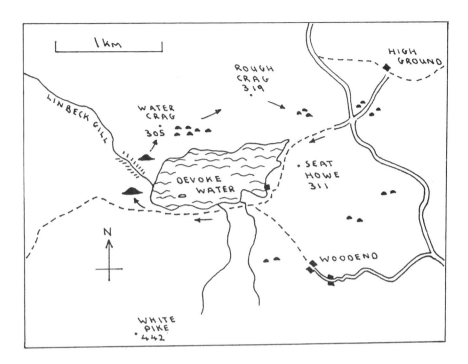

avoids the worst of it, but still the bright yellow-green sphagnum mosses and the carnivorous sundew plants grow in abundance across this short stretch before the drier slopes of Water Crag are reached. Another smaller cairn can be seen just to the left as the ground rises. This is another burial cairn but is much smaller than the first, and its less prominent position in the landscape suggest that this burial did not have the significance of the great cairn lower down. A short rocky slope takes you to the top which is marked by a large boulder and, after pausing to admire the view down to the tarn, descend towards the level col in the direction of Rough Crag.

Here on the gentle south-facing slopes is an area of many small cairns. These are probably not burial cairns, but are a result of field clearance, and are evidence that even these high slopes were used in the Bronze Age for farming. I counted at least ten, including a line of four leading down the hillside.

Where did the people who cleared this ground live? Did they live up here, or did they trek up from the valleys each day to work their small fields? Quite possibly, they would have lived for at least some of the year up on these slopes, perhaps in temporary huts which they used in the summer months when their animals grazed the high grasslands. Other, more substantial settlements might have been down in the valleys where they sheltered in the colder times of the year. Few settlement sites have been discovered so high up, suggesting that any buildings would have been built of only light materials such as animal skins.

A short climb brings you to the summit of Rough Crag, a magical place of almost white quartzite blocks and a view surpassing even the one from the burial cairn. Beyond the near fells, the great peaks clustered around Wastwater dominate the northern skyline.

Descend past the large boulder, perched precariously on the steepening slope, to the level moorland above the road. More clearance cairns can be found dotted about, and in the small triangle of land beyond the road and framed by the tracks leading to High Ground Farm, there are at least six more.

This once thriving farming area is now wild but its beauty remains untarnished. To circle the high tarn of Devoke Water and experience the peace and tranquillity of the surrounding fells is a pleasure not to be missed. Stand beside the great cairn at the foot of the lake and admire a world that is now almost lost to us.

15. The Old Man of Coniston

Approx. distance: 9 miles

Approx. time: 5 to 6 hours

Starting point: Torver G.R.283942

O.S. Outdoor Leisure Sheet: 6

Grid references: Stone circle G.R.264946; ringcairn G.R.267950; summit of The Old Man G.R.272978; ringcairn G.R.295967

Coniston Old Man is the great 'Mother' mountain of south Lakeland. Ringed by circles and cairns, it was the focal point of all the communities that lived between the mountains and the sea. Its conical shape dominates the northern horizon now as it did then, and it seems to be in view from all the ancient sites to the south.

The name 'Man' probably derives from the word 'mam' meaning 'mother', as in Mam Tor, the great sacred hill of the Peak District, and could well date all the way back to a Neolithic reverence for this, 'the old mother' mountain. Another possible meaning of 'man' is cairn, which might suggest an ancient site on the actual summit itself. This walk, passing the burial cairns and circles at its foot, and climbing up to its highest point, must surely be the ultimate pilgrimage for anyone wishing to tread in ancient footsteps.

Starting at Torver, the route begins along the walled track which starts beside the pub and winds across the fields and up through a belt of woodland onto the open fellside. The track soon becomes wet and some stepping stones prove invaluable as it crosses Bull Haw Moss.

Once firmer ground is reached, the long ridge of Bleaberry Haws rises to the left. As you approach the old slate workings, it becomes necessary to leave the path and climb up onto its grassy slopes. With the exception of one large hollowed out burial cairn down at the bottom of the southern slopes, all the sites lie on the rounded ridge line and can be easily visited one after the other.

The first is a large ringcairn, and although most of its stones are now grassed over, the bank is still quite distinct. It is about nineteen paces across and a small hump in the middle could be the remains of a central mound. About a hundred metres further on is a round cairn of rough stones with several large pieces of smooth slate which might be the rem-

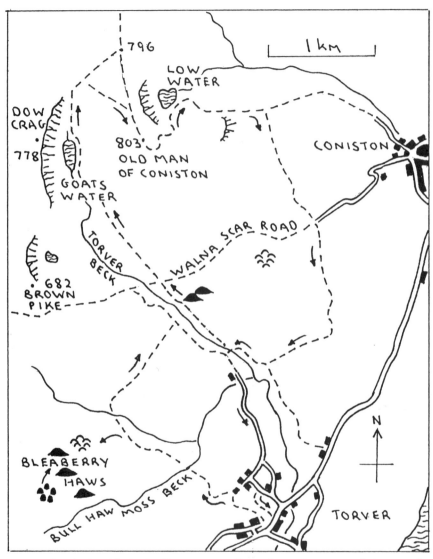

nants of a cist inside its hollow centre. From here the ground rises to the top of the ridge where another low cairn crowns the summit.

Dropping off the hill to the south-west, a tiny circle of stones soon comes into view. This must be the smallest stone circle in Cumbria, only four paces across, with none of its seven remaining stones reaching knee high.

This is a little visited moorland, and solitude is almost guaranteed. It is a place to sit and wonder, about the people who raised the stones, and how this now quiet fell must once have been alive with movement and noise. What ceremonies were once held here beside the ancient cairns and the tiny ring of stones, what pilgrims passed by on their journey to the sacred mountain rising steeply above them?

From this small circle we will now follow our own pilgrimage, back along the wide ridge of Bleaberry Haws. From the cairn on the top, look to the next one and then lift your eyes to the skyline and you will see that they are aligned perfectly with the summit of the Old Man.

The Old Man, the great 'mother mountain' of southern Lakeland.

Carry on down, past the ringcairn to rejoin the path near the old quarry workings, and follow it, between the wall and the steepening slopes of Brown Pike, until the steep-sided ghyll of Torver Beck is reached. Scramble down to the stream, choose a place where the stepping stones seem flattest and cross to the far bank.

On the low ridge just above are the remains of two more cairns. The first is quite large, of small grassed-over stones, while the second is smaller but with a ring of large kerb stones which seem out of proportion with the size of the cairn.

From here the route turns upwards and it follows the rising path to the right of the stream into the high combe between the Old Man and Dow Crag. As you climb, the great cliffs of the latter rise dramatically over the shoulder of the hill until at Goat's Water their full majesty is revealed. Soaring buttresses, rising up to lofty spires, are split by deep gullies. An immensity of grey rock, streaked with harsh black shadows, rears up above the screes and the dark waters of the tarn. Ravens tumble in the sky above and the sound of stonefall echoes hauntingly between the walls of the great amphitheatre. This of all places must have made the ancients feel that they were at last approaching the realm of their gods.

Beyond the tarn, the path steepens again, ascending the rocky slopes to the col at Goat's Hause. It then bears right around the head of the valley until the final ridge narrows and climbs to the summit. A modern cairn, conical and beautifully made, sits on top of a much older rectangular platform, and it is unlike any other mountain top in Britain.

'A modern cairn, conical and beautifully made, sits on top of a much older rectangular platform, and it is unlike any other mountain top in Britain.'

Ignore the worn paths and the people, and take in the enormity of the view, Coniston Water shining like a jewel below and the lesser fells falling away to the distant sea. To the north all the mountain ranges of the Lake District are arrayed rank upon rank to the far horizons. Treasure the moment for this was the great 'mother mountain', the natural temple to which the circles and cairns paid homage.

Whether there was indeed an ancient cairn built up there, or the summit remained an inviolate sanctuary of the gods we will never know. But it is possible to imagine the awe in which our ancestors would have approached the top of this sacred mountain.

The route down, although indistinct at first, is the safest and most popular. Descend the stony ridge which zig-zags eastwards to Low Water and then down the path through the old quarries. Below the levels and spoil heaps a broad track leads off to the right and crosses the slopes to meet the Walna Scar road.

In the moorland beyond the road is another ringcairn, tricky to find, hidden in a clearing in the bracken. It is almost identical to the one on Bleaberry Haws, nineteen paces across and with the remains of a central mound.

Returning to the path, it follows a wall to a large sheepfold, then over a stile and down to the first belt of trees. This woodland clings to a narrow ridge of rock, running away to the south-east. Clamber along its undulating top, above an area of wonderfully gnarled Tolkienesque hawthorn trees, to a wall which is crossed by a stone-stepped stile and back to Torver Beck.

Disappointingly for tired legs, it is necessary to turn back upstream for a short distance to the old quarry where the stream can be crossed and a bridleway taken back down to the village. The short section of main road can be avoided by a path across the fields leading to the church.

Go to the Old Man when the weather is settled, but avoid the week-end crowds of the summer, and always remember that its summit ridge is a high point in all senses. Treat this great mountain with respect, just as it would have been all those thousands of years ago.

16. Woodland Fell

Approx. distance: 7 miles

Approx. time: 3 hours 30 mins (9 miles and 4 hours 30 mins with Beacon Tarn.)

Starting point: Blawith G.R.288884

O.S. Outdoor Leisure Sheet: 6

Grid references: Giants Grave G.R.257879; longcairn G.R.251883; White Borran cairn G.R.266891; Beacon Tarn cairn G.R.273904

Leaving the main road at Blawith Church, follow the narrow lane westwards. It winds gradually up between the fields, past the farm at Houkler Hall, and out onto the open fell. The unfenced lane now meanders pleasantly around rocky outcrops to its end at Tottlebank. Behind the farm a bridleway continues, contouring around the southern slopes

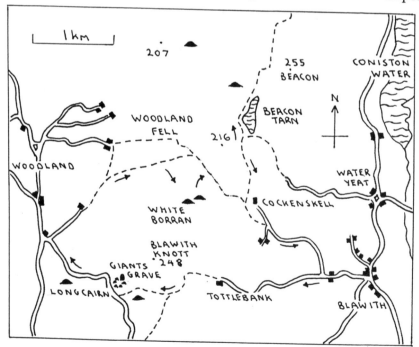

of Blawith Knott and up to a low col between the main hill and its outlier of Long Rigg. The remains of several partially grassed-over cairns
can be found beside the path. These are small, and probably the result
of ancient field clearance rather than burials. Beyond them, the track
drops down to a road climbing steeply from the village of Woodland.

Beside the road is the Giant's Grave. In reality it is a kerbed cairn
with a large standing stone at one end. Many of the kerb stones are
almost grassed over but the standing stone, despite leaning slightly
inwards, stands up proudly. Almost all the interior cairn material has
gone, leaving just a large hollow in the centre. From end to end it is
about six paces long, which no doubt accounts for its local name.
Despite the proximity of the road, it is a peaceful spot and the view
across the Kirkby Valley towards the craggy Dunnerdale Fells is worth
the walk in itself.

Below lies the very flat and marshy coastal plain which stretches for
about five miles to the coast at Duddon Sands. In Neolithic times the sea
would have reached almost up to the foot of the slopes below. As the
estuary has silted up the sea has retreated leaving the area around
Woodland high and dry.

It has long been known that the Neolithic and Bronze Age people of
Lakeland traded with Ireland because a number of the stone axes from
the axe factory at Langdale have been found there. Many more have
been discovered on The Isle of Man which probably served as a staging
post on the long and hazardous journey. In the opposite direction came
copper and gold. Gold in small quantities to fashion into jewellery and
later copper to mix with tin from Cornwall to make bronze. Other less
tangible things came too. The style of artwork, which began in Ireland
and is exemplified by the famous carvings on the kerbstones at the massive tumulus of New Grange in County Meath, later reached Cumbria.
Good examples can be found at Long Meg and Little Meg near Penrith
amongst other places.

One of the most obvious places where coastal and seagoing boats
could have landed is at the head of this large sheltered estuary. Perhaps
from there an ancient trackway would have climbed up past this old
burial cairn before crossing the low hills and on towards the great circles further north.

Leaving the circle behind, regain the road and follow it down across
the hillside towards Woodland. After it crosses a small stream and
climbs over a low ridge, several interesting cairns can be found about a

'Beside the road is the Giant's Grave, in reality a kerbed cairn with a large standing stone at one end.'

hundred metres away from the road to the southwest. They are side by side above the stream, and while the nearest is quite small and round, its neighbour is much larger and is probably a longcairn.

Back on the road the route continues almost to Yeat House before a bridleway climbs again away to the north-east. For the next mile and a half the track rises gradually above the farmland and out onto the open fells with glorious views away to the Old Man of Coniston, the great 'mother mountain' of southern Lakeland. The walking is easy underfoot as you wind across the rock-strewn hillside, moorland birds are everywhere, and the pass at High Kep is soon reached.

The path levels out and a small kerbed cairn can still just be made out beside the track as it drops away from the col. Several hundred metres further on, and before the steep descent begins, strike out onto the moors to the south, into a narrow valley. Beside the stream, in a beautiful secluded setting is a small round cairn. About fifty metres beyond it, and higher up the valley side is the White Borran, a large hol-

*'In the beautiful secluded setting is the White Borran, a large hollowed-out cairn,
built into a small, natural rock outcrop.'*

lowed cairn built into a small natural rock outcrop. This is a wonderfully peaceful place away from paths and people, with distant views
across to the Furness Fells, and is well worth the time spent searching
for it.

Following the stream back down, which is decorated with tiny primroses in April, the path can soon be rejoined as it drops down to reach
the farmland at Cockenskell. It is possible, from here, to divert up the
well-marked Cumbrian Way northwards to Beacon Tarn, where
another cairn can be found on the rugged slopes above it. Alternatively,
carry on downhill to reach a tiny lane which will lead you back to
Blawith.

This is a lovely walk throughout, easy underfoot, and although the
ancient sites are never spectacular, the marvellous views and the time-
less atmosphere of these quiet fells make it well worthwhile.

17. Sunkenkirk

Approx. distance: 7 miles

Approx. time: 4 hours

Starting point: Duddon Bridge G.R.197883

O.S. Outdoor Leisure Sheet: 6

Grid references: Sunkenkirk G.R.172882; Ash House stones G.R.193873

At Duddon Bridge the river leaves the hills and widens out into its broad marshy estuary. A short way up the narrow lane to the west of the river, an old bridleway leads through the woods past the ruins of the old Duddon Ironworks and up steeply until it levels out onto the open moor.

This is a quiet and empty landscape, away from the well-known tourist routes, and as the path crosses the lower slopes of Barrow Hill only the sound of skylarks will disturb you as meadow pipits and wheatears flit between the stones. The views are extensive, especially to the north-east where the distant summit of the Old Man of Coniston sits broodingly behind the sharp-edged shoulder of Dow Crag.

Passing a sheepfold and a cave in the rocky hillside, the path climbs steadily up, skirting around the remote farm of Thwaite Yeat to reach the high moorland road. Crossing this, a faint track leads up onto the edge of Corney Fell and around to the south of Mere Crags, where adders are common on its south-facing rocks. It is then possible to contour around the valley head to where a path drops down to Fenwick Farm. The route continues to a footbridge over the pretty Black Beck and on to Swinside.

Just beyond the farm is possibly the most impressive of all the Lakeland stone circles, Sunkenkirk. Exactly why it was sited here we will never know, but a more peaceful and tranquil place it is difficult to imagine. To the west sits the great bulk of Black Combe and its outlying fells. This great fell is at the very centre of an area rich in prehistoric sites. At least six stone circles once ringed the hill, although most have sadly been destroyed. The standing stones of the Giant's Grave still face it to the south and many cairns are scattered about its more gentle northern slopes. To the south of the circle is the small but distinctive

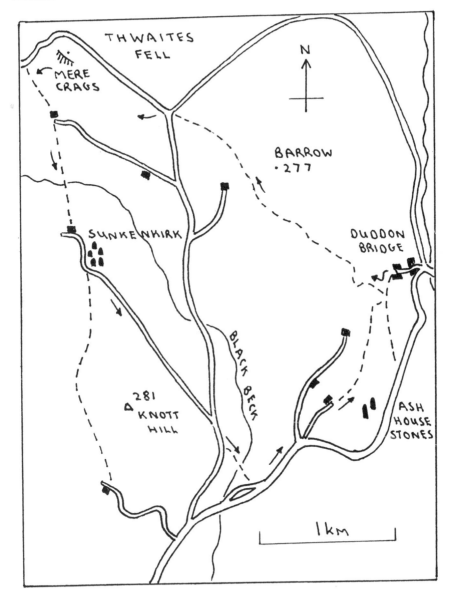

shape of Knott Hill, while away to the north-east the mountains of the
Coniston range fringe the horizon.

Built on a levelled platform most of the stones still stand, fifty-five of
a possible sixty remaining, often so close together that they almost

touch. The greatest stones stand to the north-east of the circle but other large stones are placed at intervals around the ring. The tallest, a giant finger of beautiful volcanic rock, streaked rust-red at its weathered top, stands proud above the other stones.

Facing south-east is an entrance formed by two outlying stones matching a narrow gap between two large stones leaning slightly towards each other. Each of the stones is completely different in size and shape, but the whole appears to balance into perfect symmetry and the weathered and lichen-covered rock seems as much a part of the landscape as the hills which surround them.

Its name dates back to a legend that a great church was once built here, but the devil was so jealous of the fine building that he pulled it into the ground leaving only the bare stones of the foundations standing. This is another example of how early Christianity tried to claim an obviously pagan site as one of their own.

Leaving the circle reluctantly behind, follow the track down until

the minor road is reached. A short way along it a path leads down to a line of stepping stones over the beck. When the main road is reached a rough lane takes you back into the hills past Ash House.

Up on the hillside to the south of the path are two standing stones – low but substantial boulders sitting squatly on a col between two rises in the ridge. It has been suggested that the stones are the remains of a circle, but little evidence for that can be seen on the ground which is sloping and uneven. A rocky outcrop at one side would also seem to cut into the circumference of any ring which included the two remaining stones. One other possible solution to their siting here could be that from the steep hillside behind the stones, the two align perfectly, the smaller above the larger, with the distant summit of the Old Man of Coniston.

This great mountain is also surrounded by circles and cairns, and appears to be the focal point for much of the large settlement area of southern Lakeland. Perhaps it did indeed have significance for the

*'The tallest, a giant finger of beautiful volcanic rock streaked rust red at its weath-
ered top, stands proud above the other stones.'*

people who first erected the stones? Even if they are in fact the remains
of a circle, the two remaining stones, probably the largest, could still
have been sited to line up with the distant 'Mother Mountain.'

From Ash House the path leads back into the woods, and meanders
through the old oak and birch woodland, carpeted in bluebells in the
spring, down to the bridleway where the walk began.

This isn't the shortest or the simplest route to visit Sunkenkirk, but
the open moors and quiet paths help to clear the mind and to prepare

'From the steep hillside behind the stones, the two align perfectly, the smaller above the larger, with the distant summit of the Old Man of Coniston.'

yourself for the power of the stones, for Sunkenkirk is a special place. It is a joy to visit, to sit beside and to admire the view from. Perhaps the answer to why it was built here is simply that and will become clear to all who come to this strange and magical place.

18. Lowick Common

Approx. distance: 8 miles

Approx. time: 4 hours 30 mins

Starting point: Spark Bridge G.R.306849

O.S. Outdoor Leisure sheets: 6 and 7

Grid references: Lowick Beacon cairn G.R.287841; Knapperthaw enclosure G.R.280842; Great Burney cairn G.R.264857

Lowick Common is a peaceful backwater on the southern edge of the National Park. It is a little visited area, and several ancient cairns and strange enclosures are secreted away amongst its secluded folds and on its quiet and empty fells.

This walk starts from Spark Bridge, a small village hidden down in the valley bottom of the River Crake. Follow the road up the hill to the main A5092 and cross over onto a narrow lane which climbs up, past an

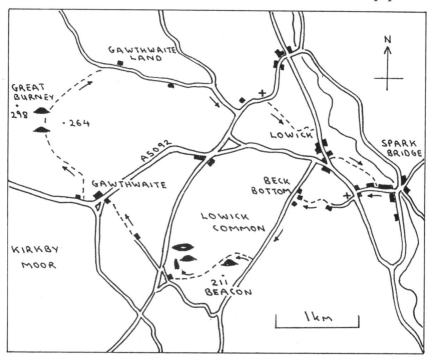

old chapel, until the road ends at Woodend. From beside the old row of cottages, a pretty walled track rises over the low hill to Beck Bottom. It is lined with harebells and red campion, and small pink germanders creep along beneath the walls. As you climb out of the valley, the great mountain ranges to the north appear beyond the lower fells.

A narrow unfenced moorland lane runs from Beck Bottom towards Lowick Beacon, the highest point of the common. Several paths wind up through the sea of bracken, curling around its northern end before climbing up to its summit ridge. There, in a clearing deep among the ferns, is a small but dramatic cairn of rough stones.

Unusually, it looks unaltered from its original shape and size, and the unrivalled views in all directions make this a very special place. Despite the presence of the narrow path it seems a little visited hilltop these days, and the unusual combination of the wide horizons with the strange and almost claustrophobic encroachment of the towering bracken, helps to create an atmosphere of remote security. It is a place to sit and let the time drift past, safe beside the old cairn, watching the clouds drift across the wide sky.

Away to the south is Morecambe Bay, while the northern horizon is dominated by the Old Man of Coniston, and at its feet Coniston Water can just be seen among the lower Furness Fells. To the west, rising over the skyline of Kirkby Moor, the slowly rotating blades of a windfarm add a rather surreal element to the magnificent view.

Dropping down the western side of the hill to the wall, a path and a walled trackway lead over a high pastureland dotted with rocky outcrops and scattered boulders to Knapperthaw. A track from the farm crosses several high fields to a small copse of trees, passing a tiny, leaning standing stone on the way. Beside the wood are the remains of a cairn and a strange ringed enclosure.

A stone bank encloses an almost level, open space about thirty paces across. The bank is mostly grassed over, but on its northern circumference several huge blocks lie on the surface. There is an entrance facing south towards the small standing stone, and one large block inside the ring which has two cup marks carved into its flat upper surface. These are small circular hollows cut into the rock and they probably had some ritual significance. They are surprisingly rare in Cumbria, for they are common along the length of the Pennines and into Scotland. In some places, such as Rombald's Moor in West Yorkshire the cups are surrounded by concentric rings and linked by other intricate grooves and channels. Whether this site was originally a banked circle from which the stones have been removed, or a type of henged enclosure is not clear, but it is undoubtedly an unusual and puzzling place.

From the farm our route follows the Cumbrian Way along a lane and over high fields back to the main road at Gawthwaite. Then it takes the road west for a short distance until a path leads out onto Gawthwaite Moor and heads for the col between the two prominent hills to the north.

After weaving around the wetter areas and crossing a tiny stream, the path climbs up onto the rocky lower slopes of the hills. Here, unusually shaped rock outcrops are emblazoned with patches of purple heather and yellow gorse, creating a strange and beautiful landscape.

As the indistinct path rises towards the col, two small clearance cairns of big stone blocks are passed, and several tall slabs of rock mark the col itself. The largest one, which stands upright and is split vertically, makes you question whether this is indeed a natural feature.

Just beyond it are the remains of a very large burial cairn. Its original size and shape can still be clearly seen although most of the stones have

been used to build a spectacular, but modern, conical cairn at one end. Again the northern view is dominated by the ever-present backdrop of the Coniston range, with the dramatic cliffs of Dow Crag deeply shadowed in the afternoon sun.

The Old Man of Coniston seems to dominate the landscape from most of the ancient sites of southern Lakeland. Standing stones align on its summit, trackways lead towards it and these high cairns all seem to have been built with it in view. The people of the time must have felt in great awe of it, and it is not surprising that it was thought of as the 'mother mountain', the great sacred hill of the area.

The walk back is long, but the constantly changing landscape and the wide views make it a pleasure and not a chore. The path drops down a wild hillside of bracken and reedbeds, where mountain hares and adders are common, to the tiny lane near Gawthwaite Land. This is followed to Lowick Church, where a path crosses the fields to Lowick Green. Another walled track contours above the river and back to Spark Bridge, where a paddle in the shallow shingles beside the bridge is a perfect end to a pleasant and interesting walk.

19. Kirkby Moor

Approx. distance: 4 miles

Approx. time: 2 hours 30 mins

Starting point: Kirkby-in-Furness G.R.230825

O.S. Outdoor Leisure sheet: 6

Grid references: burial cairn G.R.251830; ringcairn G.R.251827

Kirkby-in-Furness is a small village on the banks of a sheltered inlet off the great estuary of Duddon Sands in the south-west corner of Cumbria. Only small boats can negotiate the narrow winding channel leading from the Irish Sea these days, but it could well have been the main land-ing point for ancient boats sailing from Ireland and the Isle of Man. The centre of the village is up a low hill above the tidal pool, and it is here that our walk begins.

From the main road a quiet lane climbs gently up to Beck Side, a row of old houses beside a church which is separated from the rest of the vil-lage by several fields and a sports ground. Beyond the last house, the lane, lined with huge slate slabs, rises steeply towards the hills until a left turn takes you to Friar's Ground. When its tiny cluster of old cot-tages is reached, steps lead out onto a high field which is crossed to where a gate gives access to the open moor.

A pleasant path crosses Rot Moss, and it is worth pausing to look back and out across the tidal sands towards the distant sea. At a junc-tion of paths our walk takes the track to the right which traverses around the side of the hill. Above, the vanes of giant wind generators appear over the near skyline, surprisingly silent and graceful as they slowly rotate in the westerly breeze. Scattered across the northern end of Kirkby Moor, the wind farm dominates the moorland, but fails to destroy its wild and lonely feel.

Beside the path is what appears to be a large fallen standing stone. The long finger of rock is well weathered at one end, and beside the other, the remains of a socket in the ground in which it might once have stood. Beyond it there are the ruins of a small rectangular structure and two huge flat slabs of stone lying in the reeds alongside the track. Before long the main path approaches the shallow valley of Gill House Beck

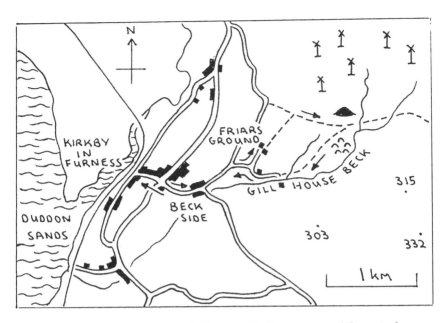

and our route turns off up the hill towards the nearest of the wind vanes, where just over the near skyline is a large burial cairn.

When it was built this must have been an imposing structure, and even today, cowed as it is beneath the huge generators, it remains impressive. It was probably a longcairn, constructed of smallish stones which, at one end, covered a stone-lined burial cist. This is now exposed as the covering of stones has been partly removed. Two large slabs near the cist could be the capping stones which have been removed, or the remains of a stone forecourt, the large stones framing the entrance to the tomb.

Who was buried here? Was it raised for one important person? Certainly, the remains of the stone cist suggests that it was, and is it significant that it sits up on this hill looking out to the west? Perhaps this person was linked with the trade across the sea, perhaps he or she came from over the water from the Isle of Man or Ireland and was buried where on a fine day the setting sun would drop down to their homeland. Whatever the reason it would have been a grand tomb, fit for a king, and even now the giant wind vanes peering over the near skyline only serve to emphasize its great antiquity.

From the cairn, drop back down the hill towards Gill House Beck. Beyond the main path are two smallish stones which stand upright, and

'the giant wind vanes peering over the near skyline only serve to emphasise its great antiquity.'

beyond them on a slight rise above the beck is a large ringcairn. A circular raised stone bank twenty-two paces across surrounds a levelled platform. Most of the stones in the bank are now hidden beneath the grass but several larger ones still can still be seen.

The purpose of these strange cairns is still a mystery, but they would appear to be more for ceremonial use rather than a place of burial. The ringcairn at Brenig in North Wales was surrounded by a circle of posts which were possibly carved and charcoal was buried in pits within the ring. It wasn't until many years later that the cremated remains of individuals were interred in the centre of the circle and beneath the ring wall. Like this one, it was also built close to cairns and tumuli and it seems logical to conclude that it was used to conduct rituals or ceremonies associated with the burial of the dead.

The track which passes between the two sites climbs directly up to here from the village and the sheltered inlet. In prehistoric times, it continued over the high shoulder of Kirkby Moor and on northwards, passing the cairns on Great Burney and Woodlands Fell in the direction of the Old Man of Coniston. From there tracks led to Langdale and over the hills to Penrith and the north. Our walk retraces the end of this ancient route down the hillside to the coast.

From the ringcairn, the narrow path drops gently down Long Moor, between the two streams, until it crosses one at a shallow ford and descends a farm track to the lane beside High Gill House. This is followed past Low Gill House to the road back to Beck Side. When the main road is reached, cross over it and down the steep hill to Sand Side beside the estuary. At the bottom of the hill, just beyond the Ship Inn is a small railway station. Cross the line over the footbridge and through a gate to reach the waters edge.

Narrow creeks and gullies wind between areas of close-cropped turf, and out on the sands, flocks of small waders probe the mud and oystercatchers wheel low over the shallow water. It must have looked the same thousands of years ago as small wooden ships, possibly with simple square-rigged sails to use the following wind, rowed in from the sea and beached on the shelving mudflats just below.

We know gold and copper was brought from Ireland, and probably landed here and further up the estuary, and that stone axes from Langdale passed the other way, but this was most likely only a small part of the trade which crossed the sea. This walk follows just a short part of this important route, but it allows us the opportunity to visit a key site in the link between the two communities.

---

20. Lacra Bank

Approx. distance: 5 miles

Approx. time: 3 hrs 30 mins

Starting point: Kirksanton G.R.139808

O.S. Outdoor Leisure Sheet: 6

Grid references: Lacra stone circles G.R.149810 and G.R.149813; stone rows G.R.152813 and G.R.151813; Giant's Grave standing stones G.R.136812

Kirksanton is a pleasant village on the flat, marshy coastal strip between the south-westerly outliers of the Lakeland mountains and the Irish Sea. Towards the coast a line of wind generators rotate gracefully in the ever present wind, while the steep fellside of Lacra Bank rises sharply from the plain.

Leaving the village towards Millom, a footpath leads over a railway line and quickly up onto the moorland beyond. This ancient trackway is deeply incised into the hillside, and thickets of gorse and wind-stunted bushes are alive with birdsong. Several small streams thread their way down the steep slope and tiny blue flowers of brook-lime grow in abundance between the rocks. Beyond the last of the stone walls, which contour around the hillside, it is necessary to leave the path to search for the first of the stone circles.

Almost immediately, you will see a small round cairn not far above the wall, barely rising now above the encroaching grass. As you climb higher the outcrops of rock increase and you enter a strange landscape of rocky hummocks and hollows. Amongst these, as the moorland levels out, is the first of Lacra's secrets.

A small ring of strangely rounded boulders nestles within the folds of the moor, hidden from all but those who seek it out. It is an almost perfect small circle in a beautifully secluded setting. The gap in it was probably filled by one of the two stones which now lie close together. Each stone has a fine textured surface and they surround an almost level platform looking out over the Duddon Sands away to the east.

From here our route climbs up the hillside towards a ruined farm-house across a heath richly carpeted in wild flowers. Tiny speedwell

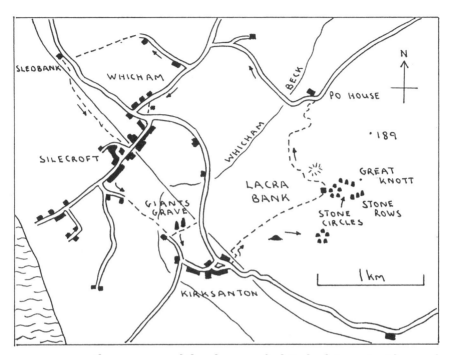

creep among the grasses and the clumps of white bedstraw. Just beyond the buildings is the second circle, sadly damaged over the years. Only four of the remaining six stones stand in their original positions, the others dumped, unceremoniously, out of the way of the faint track leading from the farmyard. Perhaps we should be amazed that it should have survived at all so close to habitation.

It is beyond this circle that the real mystery of Lacra Bank can be found. Unusual alignments of stones are scattered across the fells which do not appear to be natural. In several places they seem to be in pairs, and trace out gently curving avenues across the plateau. The stones vary greatly in size and shape and none stand particularly upright, but are these the remains of stone rows like the ones found on Dartmoor, or simple versions of the great avenues of Avebury? Whatever their original design or purpose they remain largely ruined and almost unnoticed as they trail across the heath.

Climb up onto the heights of Great Knott behind to get a better view of the complex of sites as a whole, before returning to the farm buildings and continuing the walk. The route takes the pleasant track northwards, passing the jumbled banks of an ancient enclosure to the right,

*'Unusual alignments of stones trace out gently curving avenues
across the plateau.'*

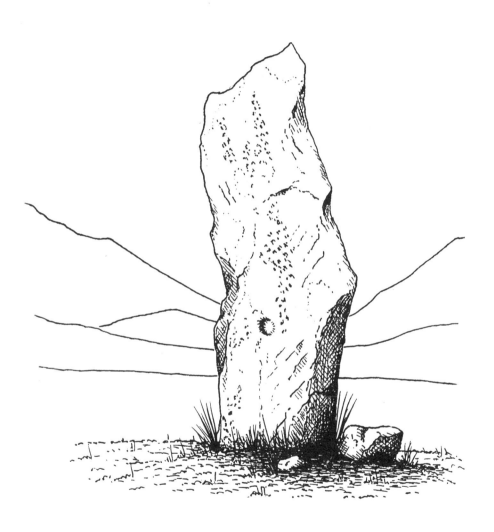

'The great blade of the taller stone points dramatically skywards between the mountains beyond.'

before dropping down ever more steeply into the Whicham Valley. As you descend, the great bulk of Black Combe blocks out the northern horizon and the rocks of Dog Crag rear up above the path.

The track meets a quiet lane at the quaintly named Po House. This is followed over Pohouse Bridge and along, between verges splashed with the colour of foxgloves and red campion, to meet the main A595. From here it is necessary to follow this busy road into Whicham before a foot-path allows you to turn off and cut down past Kellbank to the edge of Silecroft. A much longer alternative is to take the minor road to Kirkbank, and the paths past Sledbank, across the railway line to arrive in the centre of the village.

Silecroft could well get its name from the pagan sun goddess Sil, sited as it is, at the centre of such an ancient landscape. Passing through the village, a lane, signposted 'Standing Stones', leads out onto the open pasturelands beside Whicham Beck. Crossing the stream over a tiny footbridge, the standing stones of the Giant's Grave appear on the near horizon.

Tall and powerful, the two stones stand at the edge of a field, the taller over three metres high and the shorter not far short of it. Both have 'cup marks' cut into their surfaces and between them many small rounded pebbles indicate the possibility of some sort of platform beneath the grass. They align up the Whicham Valley but are turned at right angles, as if they were a giant gateway. Were they the entrance to an important area surrounding the sacred hill of Black Combe? Did they simply mark an ancient trackway along the coast, between the marshy areas on either side, or were they a monument in their own right?

Whatever their purpose, they are beautifully weathered and etched by time. Lichen creeps over their seaward-facing surfaces and the great blade of the taller stone points dramatically skywards, between the mountains beyond.

Leaving the Giant's Grave behind, return to the farmhouse called Standing Stones and a narrow lane leads quickly back into Kirksanton village.

What we see today is just the ruined remnants of a once important Neolithic area. Many of the stones have fallen or been moved, stone walls divide the monuments and the World seems to have forgotten about Lacra Bank. Fortunately, on this quiet and lonely moor, enough remains to stir our imaginations and allow our minds to recreate the impressive landscape that it must once have been.

21. Great Urswick

Approx. distance: 6 miles

Approx. time: 3 hours

Starting point: Great Urswick G.R.269746

O.S. Outdoor Leisure Sheet: 6

Grid references: Druids Circle G.R.293739; burial chamber G.R.263745; encampment G.R.274753; long barrow G.R.274754

On the southern edge of the Lake District, Great Urswick village is surrounded by limestone scars and pavements which have changed little since this was an area of great importance in Neolithic times. Many ancient sites still survive amongst the jumble of natural rock outcrops which litter the landscape.

Heading east from the village the road climbs quickly to the edge of Birkrigg Common. Footpaths criss-cross the moor, winding between

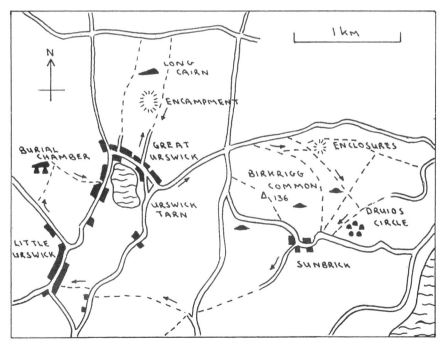

the limestone scars, and it is possible to wander at will and explore the fascinating area. The remains of a number of ancient burial cairns are scattered across the moorland including a large tumulus in a field just to the south of the common. Several strange embanked enclosures can still just be made out near the moorlands northern edge. The most obvious one is almost triangular in shape and its original purpose is now unclear.

To the east, as the common falls away towards Morecambe Bay, lies the beautiful ring of the Druid's Circle. It is in an area of scattered limestone blocks, and is not immediately easy to locate, but once found it is a little gem of a circle. Ten small stones sit in a low bank, barely eight paces across. The interior was originally levelled, and paved with 'blue rag', a stone not local to the area, but now only the sheep-cropped turf remains within the ring. The remnants of an outer ring can still be seen but what stones do remain have fallen and lie half buried in the bracken.

The stones of the inner circle are all of limestone, beautifully weathered and lichen covered, and each one completely different in shape and size. Surprisingly, all the stones are still standing, because the soluble nature of the stone often results in them breaking up. The tiny circle on Knipescar Common and the great henge at Arbor Low in Derbyshire are unfortunate examples of this. This Druid's ring remains intact however and it is an enchanting place, despite the fact that the close proximity of the road makes it one of the more regularly visited of the Lakeland circles. The view out to sea, with the morning sun shimmering on the sands of the bay only adds to the atmosphere of peace and tranquillity.

Beyond the circle is a narrow unfenced lane which crosses the Common, and this can be quickly followed into the tiny hamlet of Sunbrick. A track through a muddy farmyard brings you to an old 'green lane', which leads to another lane, from where a series of footpaths cross the fields to Little Urswick.

To the north of the village, in a strange and beautiful area of limestone scars, lie the remains of a rare exposed Cumbrian burial chamber. Two huge blocks support an equally large remnant of a capstone, although the rest of the chamber is now no more than a jumble of fallen stones. Through it all an old thorn bush grows, giving it a rather sad and forgotten air. Even the capstone has its own small windbent bush. An earth or stone mound would once have covered the chamber, but almost all trace of this has now gone – exposing it to the elements.

'. . . to the east of Birkrigg Common, as it falls away towards Morecambe Bay, lie the beautiful and evocative rings of the Druid's circle.'

The footpath from the chamber, back towards Great Urswick passes through an area of enormous, natural limestone blocks, one of which, strangely broken and eroded, is over four metres high, and several strange stone piles seem almost too chaotic to be entirely natural. It must be significant that so many ancient sites were built close to dramatic natural features such as these, indicating their importance to the people of the time. Quite likely they were the focal points of the communities before they began to construct their own monuments.

From the village a narrow lane runs northwards to a large hilltop encampment. Marked as a fort on the O.S. map it seems to have little of the great defensive banks and ditches of the Iron Age and to have more in common with the large Neolithic causewayed camps more usually associated with southern England. Natural limestone scars form three

*'Just to the north of Little Urswick village, in a strange and beautiful area of lime-
stone scars, lies the remains of a rare Cumbrian burial chamber.'*

sides of the site, but they are nowhere steep and the fourth side is just a
low bank with several apparent entrances. Such camps were probably
settlements or meeting places for the people of the area, and it is possible that it was here that traders would have come to exchange goods.

Sited as it is so close to the sea, it must be possible that it had some
connection with the important trading route between Cumbria and The
Isle of Man and Ireland. To add weight to the possibility of its Neolithic
origin are the remains of a long barrow just to the north. The shape of
the barrow can still be clearly seen and two upright stones at one end
could either be the remains of a collapsed chamber or of a ruined forecourt. The lane is quickly followed back into the village to end the walk.

Great Urswick is undoubtedly an ancient place, even its name is
probably derived from the Neolithic goddess Ur, who is remembered in
many prehistoric place names. It is also interesting that the type of sites
here differ in many respects from those to be found in the rest of

'The remains of the ancient longbarrow at Great Urswick.'

Lakeland, and seem to have more in common with other areas of the British Isles. Is it because of the links across the sea? Did people settle here, at the very edge of Cumbria, from different cultures and communities bringing with them their own customs and ways of life? Similarly, the west coast of Wales has sites more usually associated with Ireland than its surrounding area. Whatever the reason, it is easy to understand why the ancients chose to site their circles and tombs here in these quiet and peaceful hills. When the clouds drop over the higher mountains to the north it is a fascinating area to explore, for there are many hidden secrets to search for and discover here.

22. Elva Plain

Approx. distance: 2.5 miles

Approx. time: 1 hour 30 mins

Starting point: Higham Hall G.R.185316

O.S. Outdoor Leisure Sheet: 4

Grid reference: Elva Plain stone circle G.R.177317

Elva Plain is a plateau of high upland pastures above the valley of the River Derwent which flows out of Bassenthwaite Lake several miles to the east. Higham Hall is on the quiet back road from Cockermouth which climbs up across the plain before dropping down to the lake.

Our walk starts beside the Hall along an overgrown lane to the south, past its lovely gardens, and on into Bully Woods. This small patch of mature woodland contains huge oak and beech trees which overhang the narrow lane, creating an almost tunnel-like effect. As the road drops more steeply, the trees disappear to the left, opening up views to the east across Bassenthwaite to the huge mass of Skiddaw in the distance.

As it levels off, a track climbs steeply up to the right through the trees. The route now passes through a beautiful area of ungrazed hillside, and the gradual change from the luxuriant valley woodland to the open hilltop is fascinating. This could almost be a last remnant of the great wildwood which once clothed all but the highest tops thousands of years ago.

The mature oak trees quickly thin out as the path climbs, to be replaced by stunted hawthorns and wind-bent ash trees, interspersed with dense thickets of gorse and bracken and bramble. Beneath these tiny yellow primroses and other wild flowers grow in abundance, happy to have escaped the nibbling teeth of the sheep.

It is quite easy to imagine yourself back four thousand years walking through the great forest, grazed by deer and wild cattle and pigs. Packs of wolves and brown bears would still have lived, away from the settlements, in the remoter areas. Man would have already have begun to clear large swathes of the wood, but it would still have covered much of the land, cut through only by narrow tracks like this one.

The only wildlife likely to be seen today are rabbits and the small

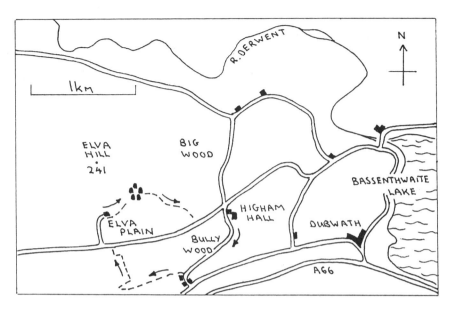

birds which sing incessantly in the thickets, and possibly a kestrel hanging in the air above the hillside. Away to the left of the path, the land rises gently before dipping to the western sea.

At the top of the slope the track doubles back and crosses several fields to reach the road, beyond which the sharp top of Elva Hill stands out. This was probably the original focal point of the plain, the natural 'hill altar' of the earlier people before the stones of the nearby circle were raised. Follow the road to the left for a hundred metres to where a farm track leads off in the direction of the hilltop. At the farm a concessionary path takes you through the yard and out into the fields beyond.

The stone circle sits in the middle of the second field. About sixteen stones remain in a circle almost thirty-two paces across. Some are grouped unusually close together while others have wide spaces between them, probably as a result of disturbance over the centuries. They are all small and rounded, and some have almost disappeared under the close-cropped turf, but the circle retains an atmosphere worth experiencing.

These days it is a peaceful place, lacking the dramatic, almost sinister feel of some circles whose jagged stones stand tall and aggressive. Whatever ceremonies or gatherings took place here thousands of years ago, these old, low, rounded boulders keep their secrets well.

'The site is very open, with wide horizons and distant views of the great mountains of northern Lakeland.'

The site is very open, with wide horizons, and distant views of the great mountains of northern Lakeland. To the east loom Skiddaw and the Caldbeck Fells, while away to the south, distant Grasmoor peers over the lower hills of the Lorton Fells.

From the stones, the well-marked path continues across several fields before dropping down to the road again. From the stile at the end of the path, the isolated hill of Binsey away to the north-east is framed by the slopes of Elva Hill and the higher trees of Saw Mill Wood. An ancient cairn crowns its summit.

A trackway once probably crossed the valley between them, before carrying on eastwards to the north of the Caldbeck Fells and on towards the settlement areas around Penrith. Such a track would have had to cross the River Derwent. A river as wide and deep as this would have been unbridgeable in those days, so a ferry would have been needed.

'An ancient cairn crowns the distant summit of Binsey.'

Simple canoes made from hollowed out tree trunks were probably used, although on some rivers, crossed by important trade routes, large rafts of thick oak planks have been discovered. Just such a raft, capable of carrying horses and even rough-wheeled carts, has been excavated at Brigg, beside the River Humber. Such boats were probably not individually owned, but shared and used communally, which shows a degree of organisation and co-operation between communities.

From the stile the road drops down into the woodland and back to Higham Hall. This is nothing but a pleasant stroll, but to approach the old circle through a last remnant of the wildwood, and to look out eastwards beyond the river to the summit cairn of distant Binsey, is like stepping back to a time long past. In early spring when the fields are full of lambs and the hedgerows shelter tiny cowslips and primroses, it is well worth a visit.

23. Blakeley Raise

Approx. distance: 6 miles

Approx. time: 3 hours

Starting point: Wath Brow, Cleator Moor G.R.030144

O.S. Outdoor Leisure sheet: 4

Grid references: Blakeley Raise G.R.061140; Great Stone G.R.066141

On the outskirts of Cleator Moor, the River Ehen flows beneath the old bridge at Wath Brow. Rising above it, the hills of Flat Fell and Dent are the most westerly outliers of the Lakeland mountains, and beyond them wild moorland stretches for mile upon empty mile. On the very edge of this wilderness is the small but beautiful stone circle known as Blakeley Raise.

Our walk begins by the river at the popular picnic spot beside the bridge, crosses it and then follows the road for several hundred metres to the north-east. Here it turns up the narrow lane which climbs towards the prominent white house high on the hillside. As it rises, the view behind, looking across the low coastal plain to the sea, widens with every step taken, until the hill levels out and the lane ends at the

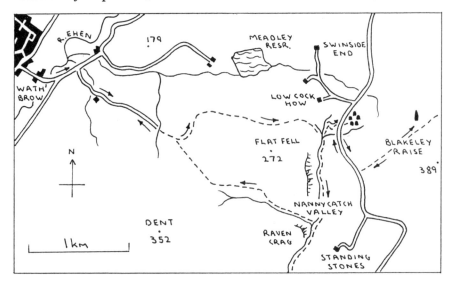

entrance to a forestry plantation. For those wishing to shorten the walk it is possible to bring a car right up to this point.

Our route ignores the forestry track and takes instead the path out onto the open moorland towards Flat Fell, then sweeps around to the north following the line of the high stone wall which forms the boundary to the fell.

As the path rises and turns to the east, a view to the wide northern horizon gradually unfolds. To the right the scree slopes of Great Bourne drop towards the hidden waters of Ennerdale Water, to the left the coast curls away to the north and ahead in the dim distance the hills of southern Scotland can just be seen beyond the lowlands of northern Cumbria.

Before long the path begins to drop, gently at first, then steeply down into the deep valley of Nannycatch Beck. The valley bottom is followed for a short way until a path can be taken to the left which climbs up and out of a side valley onto the moorland above.

Just beyond the narrow winding fell road, on a level area of grassland, eleven small stones of lichen-covered red rock stand in an almost perfect circle. They are graded in height with the tallest facing the south-east, and in the centre of the ring the outlines of a burial cairn can still be seen although it is barely more than a slight rise in the ground now.

Some doubt has been cast on the authenticity of this stone circle, but there seems little doubt that it is a genuine, if slightly restored site. Certainly the stones have been partially cemented into place, but everything else about it rings true. Its site is perfect, close to the natural springs of Nannycatch Beck, it sits on a levelled platform, with a cairn at its centre and like many other circles its largest stones stand to the south-east. It also has that unmistakable feel of a place of significance. As if to reinforce its long history, a recent memorial, partly hidden beneath one of its leaning stones, is a sad yet heart-warming reminder of the still lingering sacredness of these ancient sites.

Beyond the circle is a level area where the streams rise, and above it on the rocky hillside is a huge block of volcanic rock, probably left by the retreating glaciers of the last Ice Age. Could this be another of those natural features which became sacred to the ancestors of the circle builders, the hunters and gatherers whose wandering lives were orientated around these easily recognizable places in the landscape?

The map shows another stone over by the trees which is called the Great Stone of Blakeley, but it seems more likely that it was this one, above the circle and in full view of it, that might have influenced its siting. From the circle the sun rises directly above this stone at both the spring and autumn equinoxes, which could well have been important in determining its position. This natural altar can be easily visited by taking the road from the stones for several hundred metres to where a good track crosses the hillside towards the forest. As the trees are neared the great stone is just below, near the corner of the wood.

Stand on its flat top and look out over the stone circle, over the hills and valleys beyond to the distant sea. Did our ancestors stand on this same rock? Was it a meeting place all those thousands of years ago? Was it because of this great stone that the circle below was later built? Whatever the answers it was almost certainly from the many scattered boulders which littered the hillside here that the circle stones were selected before being rolled down the slope to the chosen site.

Returning to the road, a path can be taken just before the stream, which leads down into the Nannycatch Valley once more. From there it is a delightful walk back following the stream between steep slopes of gorse and scrub- woodland topped by the broken crags of Flatfell Screes on the western side. Before long the slopes fall away beneath Raven Crag and our walk turns up another equally narrow valley to the right. Here the path winds alongside a tiny stream which whispers its way

'Was it because of this great stone that the circle below was later built?'

down to join the Nannycatch, before climbing up and out of the valley and onto the moorland above. This is quickly crossed to rejoin the approach route which is followed back to Wath Brow.

This is a short but scenic route, to one of the few Cumbrian circles which probably looks very much today as it did thousands of years ago. The approach, out of the deep and enclosed defile of the Nannycatch Valley, to the stones on the open moorland with its wide horizons, is both dramatic and inspiring. Take your time, there aren't many short walks more enjoyable than this.

24. Sampson's Bratfull

Approx. distance: 12 miles

Approx. time: 6 hours

Starting point: Haile G.R.034086

O.S. Outdoor Leisure sheet: 4

Grid references: Bell barrow G.R.058101; henge G.R.071099; ringcairn G.R.072098; Sampson's Bratfull longcairn G.R.098080; kerbed cairn G.R.096078; enclosure G.R.061062

This is a long and, in places, difficult walk which enters one of the wildest and remotest areas of the Lake District. Once off the paths the ground is often wet and featureless and in poor weather good navigational skills are essential. Despite this, it has all the elements of a classic walk: quiet lanes, pleasant footpaths, and trackless moorland with sweeping views up empty and desolate valleys. And to cap it all, it offers the widest variety of ancient burial cairns and barrows to be found in Cumbria.

It starts at Haile, a quiet hamlet up in the low hills on the western fringe of the National Park. A lane is followed out of the northern end of the village past the entrance to Haile Hall and up over a hill before dropping down into the valley of Hannah Beck. The valley bottom is a tangled heathland of gorse bushes and scrub trees and abounds in birdlife. Buzzards wheel silently overhead and mixed groups of tits and finches flit from tree to tree beside the lane.

Before long, it reaches the high unfenced road which climbs up over the fells from Ennerdale Bridge. After crossing the road a good track leads into a shallow trough between the hills which drop away towards the deeper valley of the River Calder beyond. To the right of the path is the large natural spring called the Friar's Well, where a tiny stream bubbles up into a green and overgrown pool before spilling out and running away towards the river. Just beyond it is the first of the ancient barrows.

Looking just like a natural hillock initially, it isn't until you leave the path that it becomes clear that not only is it a man-made mound, but that it is in fact a bell barrow because it is surrounded by a shallow ditch and a low bank. This is very unusual, especially in northern England,

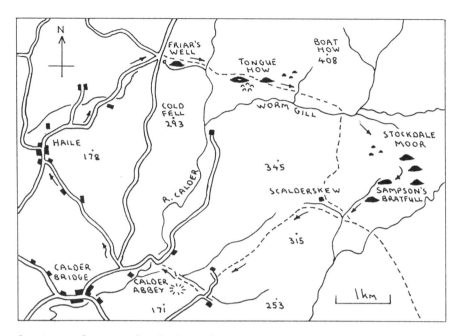

but in southern England where they are more common it often indicates a high-status burial, which is consistent with its situation so close to such a significant natural feature as the well.

Beyond the barrow the track drops quickly down to a bridge over the River Calder, and then up the slope on the other side onto the empty moorland of Tongue How. As the path levels out, a large stone feature comes into view. Marked on the map as a homestead, it is a high circular bank of rough stones the size of a large ringcairn. What is strange is the height of the stone banks which give it the appearance of a small henge, almost like a miniature version of the famous site at Mayburgh. Standing within the ring, the banks are tall enough to block out the outside world except where a narrow entrance faces north-east towards the distant hilltop of Lank Rigg.

Beyond the ring is an area of banks and scattered mounds and other strange land features, all evidence of disturbance by man and includes a large shallow pit which could well be the original quarry. About a hundred metres to the south-east is a small ringcairn which is only eight paces across, with well constructed stone banks and an entrance facing directly towards the larger circle. Several large blocks lie in a puzzling jumble inside it. This is a confusing area which poses many

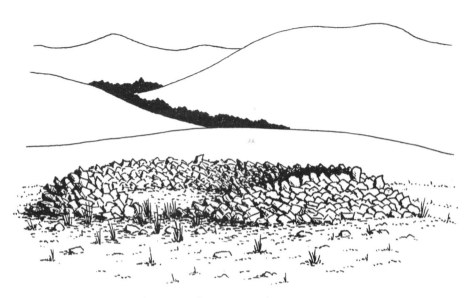

'The unusual stone ring of Tongue How.'

unanswered questions, and much time could be spent exploring it in more detail, but it is undoubtedly a site of ancient settlement and land use.

The track continues across the moor passing several more cairns until it drops down to the beautifully wild valley of Worm Gill. The river runs through wide areas of shingle banks and in some places splits into numerous channels which wind between islands of water-smoothed stones. Beside it, strange green mounds rise up from the moor where large stones have been completely grown over by mosses and alpine plants. Upstream the valley continues, empty and untouched to where its feeder streams run off Lank Rigg and the outlying fells of Haycock, dark and snow-streaked in the distance. There is a ford marked on the map, although in all but the driest periods an easier crossing can be made where the river divides into its many shallow channels.

Across the valley rises the wet and bleak fells of Stockdale Moor. No paths cross this wild area of tussock grass and reed beds and it is best to take a direct line towards the drier, higher ground beyond. When this is reached many scattered clearance cairns indicate areas of ancient field systems and a line of larger cairns runs along the crest of the moor.

Below these, a shallow valley falls away to the south-west and in it is the mysteriously named Sampson's Bratfull, which is in reality a large longcairn built over a natural spring near its head. It is at least thirty paces long, running from east to west with a narrowing tail to the west. It has many pits and hollows in its high stone banks which could be indicative of collapsed chambers within, but is more likely to be the result of past excavations. If you sit at its wider eastern end, water can be clearly heard bubbling up beneath the stones, again showing how our ancestors held such natural features as sacred and important enough for this great tomb to have been built here. This is a lonely, little-visited place and the empty moors stretch away to the east where the distant summit of Seatallan rises up, crowned with its own ancient burial cairn.

'The ancient longcairn of Sampson's Bratfull.'

Beyond Sampson's Bratfull the ground is drier, the walking more pleasant and the valley can be followed down until another large and unusual cairn is reached. This appears to be the remains of a kerbed cairn which has been built on top of a larger, levelled, stone platform. Almost all the cairn material has gone but the kerb stones are still clearly visible. This part of the moor is much drier, and the grasslands beside the small stream would have been a pleasant place to live and farm.

The shallow valley eventually leads to a track heading towards the remote farm at Scalderskew, and this is taken to where a gate gives access to a right of way up the hillside to the left of the stream. Again, the path which is marked on the map does not appear to exist on the ground until the col above the farm is reached, where it becomes a good track winding down the gentle slopes of Ponsonby Fell.

A dramatic view out to the coast and beyond accompanies this section of the walk, with Sellafield dominating the coastal lowlands and the Isle of Man hanging almost cloud-like on the western horizon. A wide ridge is followed between two streams until a farm track takes you down to a lane leading to Laverock How. Turn left and follow this to a quiet lane and almost immediately branch off on a path beside Scargreen Beck. After crossing and re-crossing the stream it enters an area of woodland and winds between mossy trees, decorated with tiny ferns, which hang over the path. Away to the left near the top of the wood are the banks of an ancient enclosure almost hidden within the trees.

As the wood ends, the stream enters a narrow sandstone gorge and the path follows it down to where it joins the River Calder near Stakes Bridge. From there the lane is taken back, past the medieval ruins of Calder Abbey, to a junction where another quiet lane winds between farms and high fields for another two miles until the walk ends back at the village of Haile.

Glossary

Avenue – a ceremonial route lined with paired standing stones, often linking stone circles with places of burial.

Barrow – an earthen mound covering a burial, usually round in shape, and dating from the Bronze Age.

Cairn – a mound of stones, often covering a burial and usually round in shape.

Cairn circle – a cairn, of which only the kerb stones remain.

Capstone – the stone forming the roof of a burial chamber or cist.

Causewayed camp – a Neolithic enclosure with many entrances which may have been a meeting or market place.

Chambered cairn – a cairn with a burial chamber, or chambers, inside it.

Cist – a stone sarcophagus usually beneath a cairn or barrow.

Clearance cairn – a cairn made up of stones cleared from land on which crops were raised and not usually associated with burial.

Clint – block forming part of a limestone pavement.

Dolmen – the exposed stones of a burial chamber after the mound or cairn have gone.

Enclosure – an area enclosed with prehistoric banks or ditches.

Forecourt – a stone-lined entrance to a chambered cairn or barrow.

Ghyll – Cumbrian term for stream

Henge – a circular enclosure surrounded by a bank which sometimes has an interior ditch.

Kerb cairn – a burial cairn where the small cairn stones are held in place by larger kerb stones around the base.

Kist – see cist

Kerb stones – a ring of larger stones around a cairn which held in the smaller cairn stones.

Long barrow – a long mound, usually dating from the Neolithic period, usually with burial chambers inside.

Long cairn, or **longcairn** – a long cairn, usually with burial chambers inside.

Megalith – a large stone, erected or positioned by man in the Neolithic or Bronze Ages.

Outlier – a standing stone positioned outside a stone circle.

Ring cairn or **ringcairn** – a ring of cairn stones with a level space inside. Originally, they were probably surrounded by a circle of timber posts and were for ceremonial rather than burial purposes.

Standing stones – stones which do not form part of a circle and which may have been waymarkers or portals.

Stone circle – a circular ring of large stones sometimes built into a low bank.

Stone row – a row of stones, often leading to or from a stone circle.

Tumulus – an old name for a barrow.

Bibliography

Gordon Barclay, *Farmers Temples and Tombs*, Canongate Books,1998.

Aubrey Burl, *A Guide to the Stone Circles of Britain, Ireland and Brittany*, Yale, 1995

Aubrey Burl, *Circles of Stone*, Harvill,1999.

Richard Cavendish, *Prehistoric England*, Artus Books, 1983.

Julian Cope, *The Modern Antiquarian*, Thorsons, 1998.

R.G. Plint, *Stone Axe Factories in the Cumbrian Fells*, Transactions, 1961.

T.G.E. Powell, *Prehistoric Art*, Thames and Hudson, 1966.

Ray Seton, *The Reason for the Stone Circles in Cumbria*, Ray Seton, 1995.

Also from Sigma Leisure:

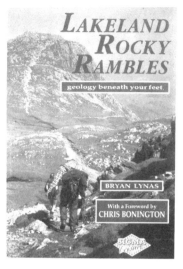

LAKELAND ROCKY RAMBLES: Geology beneath your feet
Bryan Lynas

This is both a guide to carefully-selected Lake District rambles and a detailed explanation of the rocks and scenery that you'll actually see, walk on or scramble over: real hands-on (or feet-on) science in Nature's own laboratory where you *can* touch the exhibits.

Picture the drama of an ancient deep sea which was later destroyed, the sea floor being thrust up by mighty earth movements to form mountains. Imagine volcanos spewing lava, ash and a deadly type of eruption which man had never witnessed. Discover how the whole district froze solid, buried by grinding ice sheets which melted just 11,500 years ago. To add to your pleasure, you'll find notes on the birds, plants and fungi you may see. Jargon is avoided, though you'll find any necessary geological words explained in a Glossary. £9.95

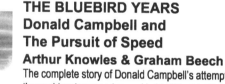

THE BLUEBIRD YEARS
Donald Campbell and
The Pursuit of Speed
Arthur Knowles & Graham Beech

The complete story of Donald Campbell's attempts to raise the world water-speed record in his "Bluebird" jet-propelled boat to 300mph. Includes the dramatic recovery of "Bluebird" from Coniston Water and the intrigue that surrounded the operation. Features dramatic photographs, close-ups of "Bluebird" and shots of record attempts at full speed. Ken Norris, designer of Bluebird, presents a reconstruction of the causes of the accident and an account of the recovery of the wreck. £9.95

IN SEARCH OF SWALLOWS & AMAZONS: Arthur Ransome's Lakeland
Roger Wardale

A new edition of a popular book originally published in 1986. Additional material has been added to satisfy even the most avid reader of "Swallows & Amazons" – three decades of

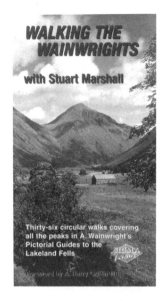

Ransome hunting with text and photographs to identify the locations of the ever-popular series of books. There's a two fold pleasure in this book – enjoying the original stories and discovering the farms, rivers, islands, towns and hills that formed their backdrop. £7.95

WALKING THE WAINWRIGHTS
Stuart Marshall
This ground-breaking book is a scheme of walks linking all the 214 peaks in the late Alfred Wainwright's seven-volume Pictorial Guide to The Lakeland Fells. After an introduction to the Lake District, the route descriptions are clearly presented with the two-colour sketch maps facing the descriptive text - so that the book can be carried flat in a standard map case. The walks average 12 miles in length but the more demanding ones are presented both as one-day and two-day excursions. £7.95

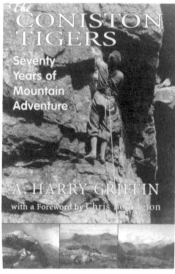

THE CONISTON TIGERS:
seventy years of mountain adventure
A Harry Griffin
As much of interest to lovers of the great outdoors as to those who simply enjoy writing of the highest calibre, "The Coniston Tigers" features period photographs of climbers from the 1930s with their minimal climbing gear – some nonchalantly smoking their pipes as they balance on the most delicate ledge. "A very special book . . .a living history of Modern Lakeland climbing" – Chris Bonington. "Harry Griffin is one of the great outdoor writers of the century" – Cameron McNeish, Editor of The Great Outdoors. £9.95

All of our books are available through booksellers. In case of difficulty, or for a free catalogue, please contact: SIGMA LEISURE, 1 SOUTH OAK LANE, WILMSLOW, CHESHIRE SK9 6AR.

Phone: 01625-531035   Fax: 01625-536800.

E-mail: info@sigmapress.co.uk
Web site: http//www.sigmapress.co.uk

MASTERCARD and VISA orders welcome.